What Makes a
Wine Worth Drinking

ALSO BY TERRY THEISE

Reading Between the Wines

What Makes a
Wine Worth Drinking

———

IN PRAISE OF THE SUBLIME

———

Terry Theise

HOUGHTON MIFFLIN HARCOURT
BOSTON   NEW YORK
2018

For information about permission to reproduce selections from this book, write to trade.permissions@hmhco.com or to Permissions, Houghton Mifflin Harcourt Publishing Company, 3 Park Avenue, 19th Floor, New York, New York 10016.

hmhco.com

Library of Congress Cataloging-in-Publication Data
Names: Theise, Terry, 1953– author.
Title: What makes a wine worth drinking : in praise of the sublime / Terry Theise.
Description: Boston : Houghton Mifflin Harcourt, 2018. | Includes bibliographical references.
Identifiers: LCCN 2018012317 (print) | LCCN 2018014722 (ebook) | ISBN 9781328761958 (ebook) | ISBN 9781328762214 (hardcover)
Subjects: LCSH: Wine and winemaking.
Classification: LCC TP548 (ebook) | LCC TP548 .T49 2018 (print) | DDC 641.2/2 — dc23
LC record available at https://lccn.loc.gov/2018012317

Book design by Allison Chi

Printed in the United States of America
DOC 10 9 8 7 6 5 4 3 2 1

Some material was originally published in slightly different form in the magazine *World of Fine Wine*.

The pleasure of seeing into the life of things is one of the least celebrated and most important of the panoply of satisfactions.

—Rebecca Solnit

CONTENTS

What Makes a
Wine Worth Drinking

INTRODUCTION

We are set down on this earth bewildered. Myself right now, I am completely bewildered. Someone asked me once why I write and I replied, "Because I cannot speak and cry at the same time."

—Tom Spanbauer

I buy produce at the same farmers' market each week. I've gotten to know the farmers, so that when I eat a meal it's not just tomatoes or even heirloom tomatoes, it's Helen's tomatoes or Jeff's eggplants or Kathy's thyme. And because the growers know me, too, I like to imagine that from time to time they think of me when they pick an especially sweet ear of corn or plum tomato: "Terry will like this."

In much the same way, I have been fortunate enough to develop strong relationships with some very talented vintners. And when I taste their wines, I can't help but think of them, and of their vineyards.

The best wines are infused with the spirits of the people and places that produced them. This is a simple truth that I was lucky enough to learn very early in my wine-drinking life. The growers I met during my earliest days of becoming seriously interested in wine showed me the wines they had made, told me about the soils their wines were grown in, poured samples for me, and encouraged me to explore the vineyards. Often they came along. (A few of them must surely have wondered how a young man who looked more at home behind a drum kit than in a tasting room had ever darkened their doors. Years of fussing from many people in my life had never convinced me to cut my [very long] hair, but after that first trip to visit growers, I had to; I didn't want to freak them out.)

Wine was presented as a being with a life equivalent to mine, not as a "thing" to be examined and judged. Of course I had preferences, but I never felt superior to wine. It came from grapes that grew in living soil. It was made by living people who tilled their land as gardeners till their gardens, with attention and respect and concern. Wine was a citizen of eternity, just as I was, and as we all are.

My relationship with wine was a conversation between two living beings. This was imprinted on me from the start, and has become my paradigm, my template for being with wine. It isn't a "hobby," it isn't something I look upon from a place of remove—it's telling, I think, the popular publication's title, *Wine Spectator*. It is rather a companion, has always acted companionably, and has never let me down.

My phrase "living being" can muddy the waters, I know. Wine isn't sentient. But it is biologically alive and chemically active, and when it is anchored to its place of origin and to its producer's intimacy with those places, I find it has a *self*. It possesses an existential reality that makes it more than merely a thing. The same can be claimed by cheesemakers and even by potters, I'm sure you would agree. A beautifully made work of pottery is both an object and an expression of the hands, eyes, and soul of the person who formed it.

If we see the world "sacramentally" (in Anne Lamott's coinage), then we live among a host of beings aglow with life force. If we see the world materially, we live in a kind of poverty.

Any authentic wine can glow with this life force. What makes a wine authentic? I'll tell you. It can't be a "consumer good" and it can't be made industrially, because then it really is a "thing" that's just like every other thing by which consumers are induced. Authentic wine is connected to place and family, whatever that may entail. It is not "formed" to appeal to a "market."

If we see wine as a being and not a thing or an "item" or a product, that view changes everything. The drinking of wine becomes a dance of equal beings instead of the consumption of an entertainment. I find that the question of authenticity is the first principle; it comes before I taste and judge whether I like a wine and how much. If a wine is inauthentic, I'd rather not know it at all. It's a guy I don't wanna hang out with.

I also consider, why this particular friend? What makes him a good companion? Concomitantly, what would make him an annoying one? My friends are selected to the extent they please me, before I step back to contemplate and respect their more serious attributes. And so the basic question: by what am I pleased or displeased? I have learned I prefer friends who are easy to be with. They aren't always my most fascinating friends, but sometimes I prefer ease and solace to fascination. There are wines that show an unseemly assertiveness, as if they are afraid I won't hear them. I hear them just fine—I simply don't like them. (I have rather an uneasy friendship with so-called natural wines; sometimes I love them and other times I want to cringe. They make exceptionally scintillating conversation, but they forgot to apply deodorant. If we arrive at a place where flaws and unpleasantness are *proof* of authenticity, we are letting ourselves be abused. More on this later.)

If I am in a relationship with wine, I must consider whom I bring to the dynamic. I must think about myself. At the same time I must engage with the wine as a fellow being, but a separate being. It (or "he" in many European languages) is not me. What do I see through my windows? What is actually there? And what is the most useful and telling way to describe this? Seeing wine as a being—or as a friend—asks us to think about the question of objectivity. After all, we're not objective about our friends, even if we can enumerate their virtues. We may well admire them, but we're friends because we like them. We have a dual vision. We examine our own filters and assumptions and are compelled to examine why we like the wines we like. Where are the lines between subjective and objective? Are there lines at all? If we indeed possess dual vision, what do we see out of each eye?

I will try to tell you.

If I am in a relationship with wine, it stands to reason this will change as I myself change. Getting older entails a reordering of one's position on mortality, which is to say, it becomes real. Our very voices change. The things we talk about are different now. My relationship to beauty becomes more crucial, as many things do. Wine is a being of beauty, addressing parts of me that weren't there before. This needs to be understood, but first it must be acknowledged and described.

Finally, if wine is indeed a fellow being, it can never be an object I place into a box to pull back out when I want to play with it. It is an inextricable part of my life, and even more: it is an inextricable part of *life*. As I go about my days, even when I'm not thinking of wine, it is present. It's a free-range sort of friend; it touches what it pleases and lets itself be touched back. It orbits my other concerns and is orbited by them. It makes me think of other things, and other things make me think about wine. There is no separation between this and that. I will say what it's like to live this way, especially but not exclusively when I'm on tasting trips to select for my professional portfolio. Life, it turns out, is wonderfully rich and strange and lovely.

Let me put this in the form of what I shall fatuously call a "manifesto" but which is merely an outline of ideas on which I myself presume, but which may not be self-evident to you, dear reader.

Small-scale family-produced wine is always preferable to large-scale industrially produced wine. This value judgment is fundamental to how I understand wine. It is only indirectly related to the "quality" of wines. This can be misconstrued. In my frame of reference, the origin of a wine precedes any judgment as to its quality. There are consumers who insist, "I don't care who made a wine or how or what size the winery was; I just want it to rock my world." I don't agree. The value of artisanality precedes the value of quality, though both, of course, are abiding values.

Noisy wines, that is, wines that really holler their flavors, are to be avoided because they contribute to the general coarsening of our somatic lives and ultimately to the nature and quality of our thought and discourse.

Beauty of flavor is more important than impact of flavor, just as harmony is more important than intensity.

The finest wines are distinctive; they display their origins with the greatest possible clarity and detail. This glimpse of place is part of the spirit of place, and when we let ourselves respond to that spirit, it helps us locate ourselves and our lives.

Clarity of flavor is itself the very first principle of wine, because when it is absent we struggle to view a wine's other attributes.

Your "palate" is only partly your sensory grasp of flavor; it is more saliently the entire sensibility you bring to aesthetic experience.

Language is notoriously inept at describing flavor, yet this very phenomenon is a useful vector into experiences some people view as mystical or soulful.

Consumerist wine writing, for all it is useful to "consumers," is ultimately suffocating to both the wine and the reader. This does not apply to informational or journalistic wine writing, which is essential, but which isn't the sine qua non of engagement with wine.

Wine is, at its best, an agent of beauty, and the writer does well to engage with it on that level. Does well and looks foolish. The older writer is less perturbed by looking foolish than his younger self was. He is also more mindful of how crucial beauty is. For a young person, beauty is most often lyrical, but for a white-bearded dude like me, beauty is an uneasy reminder to love the world I will soon be leaving.

And then you start to write, and then it all goes to hell. Where are the words when you need them?

I suppose if they arrayed themselves in tidy multitudes in front of me, I could defy centuries of philosophy and create the ultimate text about beauty. But no, the words are like mice in your walls; you hear them only at night, and in the morning they are hidden once more. Thus the discursive form can be a helpful means to hew any sort of pathway, to walk through these thick wild woods. And to do this, we need a larger view of wine than the prevailing literature provides.

In this book I approach the subject of wine with two lenses, a narrow-angle lens that will seek to explain the values that make one wine preferable to another, and a wide-angle lens through which we can start to consider why any of this matters at all.

Wine is not a self-contained universe, but if we write as though it were, we run a bunch of risks. One, it can seem precious. Two, it can feel suffocating. Three, it puts a distance between the reader—a warm-blooded he or she—and the object, wine—an it. The problem with much wine writing, even good wine writing, is that it doesn't know what it ought to be doing. Wine is a key that unlocks a door, but too many wine writers walk through the door thinking they're in the house, whereas they've merely walked into a vestibule, where bottles of wine sit upon a table and mirrors are on all the walls, so that no matter where they look all they see are wine bottles and themselves looking at wine bottles, repeated and reflected into infinity as though that were the sum of existence. Meanwhile, the house beyond this little anteroom is pulsing with life.

The prevailing "wine literature" (which is seldom literature at all) has done a laudable job of laying out information about various wines: their origins and upbringings. It also offers suggestions of what wines you ought to buy at varying budgets. It also wants you to know how "simple" wine is. All of this is useful, and all of it starts by assuming that you, helpless reader, are quaking with inadequacy when dealing with—*gulp*—wine.

A micro-focus on arcane technicalities erects yet another membrane between wine and the person who seeks to know about it. Too much wine writing also seems to crawl into an envelope and seal it from the inside. It's as though a writer discussed his cross-country journey by writing only about the engine of his car, what his mileage was, how often he checked his tire pressure. He doesn't even say what music he played! Landscapes whiz by unremarked upon. "On the climb up the front range of the Rockies my motor was really purring; I gave it 94 points on my 100-point scale."

There's a secret we "wine people" know, and it is that everyone else hates us. I remember sitting with a group of tasters who were tormenting some hapless wine, and one guy said, "This really smells like pears," and another guy said, "Really? I get more peaches . . ." and a third person said, "Maybe like Comice pears, one of the sweeter ones," and a girl said—I am not inventing this—"Yeah, but from the shady side of the tree, where the acid's higher."

Anyone who's ever sat around with other wine folk is nodding in rueful recollection. Of course it's harmless, sort of, and yet if it were a YouTube video its title could be "Why Everyone Hates Wine Snobs," even if these people were not actually snobs. We're just members of a club; we have our runes and arcana, our lingo and our cultural assumptions. What we too seldom have is any sense of the rest of the world.

Even more perilously, we often seem to lack any sense of our own interior worlds. We become life-support systems attached to "palates." We become, in a strange sense, machines, seeking some pure depiction of the wine-object in all its detail yet deliberately ignoring our internal landscapes; wine becomes an inert specimen we depict. This is fine if we are your cardiologist listening for a heart murmur, but perhaps less apropos when engaging a being of beauty. Sure, people in any profession get together and talk shop, but not all shops are created equal; widgets are one thing and wine is another. Considering all the lip service we pay to wine as an element of a gracious and civilized lifestyle (that hateful word!), I'd argue that we pay too much attention to style and not enough to *life*.

We need, that is, to consider the many shoots and tendrils wine sends out. To some modest degree this too has been done, not often, but often enough to be helpful. Wine, after all, bears on issues of chemistry, geology, microbiology, agriculture, culture in general, family, and conviviality. If wine were merely a bringer of sensual pleasure and intellectual curiosity, it would almost be enough. But wine also bears upon questions of morality (in terms of its honesty), upon conscience (prominently but not exclusively environmental), and upon the nature and purpose of beauty. And then we are up to our shoulders in mystery.

This is where most wine writing turns back. Doing so is an error of timidity, to yield at the doorway of the ineffable, but I understand. This stuff is the very devil to write about, and you can easily look like a fool. But I'm ever more convinced that it is just from this point that the most crucial writing about wine can begin. And I don't mind if I look silly or pretentious. Those vanities are long since shed.

Let's put it this way: There are two ways to write about the heavens. One of them is scholarly; it is about astronomy. The other is poetic; it is about the feelings one has while considering the stars. In wine we have a similar schism; we can write about it cerebrally and analytically, or we can write about the imaginative places it may escort you to. I like the English habit of writing about one's hobbies and pleasures with appreciation. An Englishman might write a book called *My Life as I Looked at the Stars,* and even if you didn't care very much about the stars, you'd read the book because the narrator is so engaging. But most Americans would wrestle the subject to the ground with obsessive detail before proceeding to rate the constellations on a 100-point scale.

Clearly I prefer one approach to the other. In my earlier book, *Reading Between the Wines,* I wanted to establish a basic architecture of values about wine. That is, if we think about wine in terms of its rootedness to families and culture, we're reminded of our own rootedness (or rootlessness for some of us), and if we cherish the attentiveness permitted by making wine in small batches, we learn that we can taste it. And with this third eye of our palates opened, we learn the joys of wines radiant with clarity, distinctiveness, grace, balance, deliciousness, complexity, modesty, persistence, and paradox.

I tried to answer the question "Why care at all about wine?" And having done it—or failed to do it if you hated the book—I sought to demonstrate what a person's relationship to wine might be with that new frame of reference in place. It felt like a good place to summarize how I had "lived" wine, but I knew I wasn't finished. Because wine won't ever be finished, because its deepest secrets cannot be *known,* they can only be worried and poked at and mulled over. Yet in all this mulling and musing something of value occurs, and even if this is nothing more than the squirming cogitations of a mind engaging with beautiful unanswerable questions, I am sure it is worth sharing.

In our go-go culture we risk losing the benefits of reverie, or even of ordinary daydreaming. Great wine can induce reverie; I imagine most of us would concur. But the cultivation of reverie is also the best approach to understanding fine wine at all. Blaise Pascal wrote, in his *Pensées,* "All of humanity's problems stem from man's inability to sit quietly in a room alone." My interpretation: only by cultivating such stillness can we receive everything wine has to give.

In its highest form, wine offers us a doorway into a country of musings and dreams. I live near the Forest Hills cemetery in Boston, and it is a sylvan place, a classic New England cemetery; e. e. cummings and Anne Sexton are buried there, and huge old trees shade the stones and the statuary, and there is even a pond populated by geese and ducks, and if you're lucky you might spot the occasional heron or tortoise browsing among the reeds. My wife and I love to walk there. Someone might wonder why we expose ourselves deliberately to something so gloomy, and it's hard to know how to respond except to say that the sadness I feel is actually very sweet. I come away tender, grateful, calm, and somber. I feel cleansed of bitterness and free of small things. And certain wines make me feel exactly like that.

I suppose I'm lucky to have a mind that makes connections and laces them together. Often when feeling one thing, I think of other times when I felt similarly. It might seem a a little jarring to use space in a "wine book" to talk about cemeteries and (coming right up!) dachshunds, but how else do we enfold the feelings wine can engender into the whole of our lives?

So, we dog-sat a few weeks ago. Dimmy is a long-haired dachshund who is about the softest dog you ever held. And he loves being held. One of the commands he responds to is "Come cuddle," and if I were lying on the couch it wouldn't be long before Dimmy jumped up and curled his sweet-smelling self up against me. He'd even put his head on my chest, or in the crook of my arm with his snout up against my neck. (He was also fiendishly adept at placing himself perfectly between me and any book I may have been trying to read.) One time I was aware he was dreaming; his breathing quickened and I watched his eyes move, and I thought, *What would I do if he woke up from a nightmare?* (Do dogs have nightmares? They have to, right?) Suddenly I was flooded with feeling. Of course I'd try to console him if he woke up from a bad dream, this warm little being sleeping so trustingly in my arms.

And certain wines make me feel exactly like that.

There seems to be a sort of home in our hearts and souls for beautiful things—music, poetry, wine, baseball, whatever one happens to find beautiful. But since this is at least proximately a wine book, the language of wine will be the glide path into the discussion. When I switch lenses from narrow to wide angle, especially as the book flows into its latter half, there may be pages at a time where wine seems to disappear. But it will come back, because it is always there, and that is because beauty is always there. That's what happens when you're not obsessed with wine but when you simply love it.

I have a special affection for the wines in the middle; they aren't the cheapest and they aren't the biggest; they're just delicious, useful, and charming. Right, I know: poo on that. We don't "drink" wine, and if we do we certainly don't waste any mental bandwidth on how "delightful" or "delicious" it might be. That is for nimrods. We appraise our wines; it's a kind of blood sport. We judge and evaluate and we especially pay terribly close attention to how the wine makes *us* look; will our industry pals respect us? Does our wine kick sand in the other wine's face?

Is it enough for a wine to be unique and wonderful? Doubtful. Is the sweet-natured moderation of these in-between wines something we might respond to? Nah, it isn't noisy enough. Does the nature of the flavor matter in the least? You must be joking.

Are we at risk of perverting the very reasons we ever got into wine at all? *Yes, we are.*

I remind you of some of those reasons in the pages that follow—and also offer some new ones. To begin, I offer you a bit of autobiography, when it pertains to how my approach to wine was formed. I didn't just magically become the wizened old sage whose book you hold in your hand. That great saying "We don't see the world the way it is; we see it the way we are" may have been first said by Anaïs Nin or Dale Carnegie, but either way it's worth remembering.

Along with identifying the sources of my profound and unfathomable weirdness, I focus a narrow-angle lens on wine. Two things will transpire: I explain some of the larger debates taking place in the wine world and why some of them are threats to wine itself, and I also build a basic foundation for the application of a system of values. That is, what wines are crucial and what wines are ancillary, why wine matters in the first place, how wine is to be judged humanely (from the entirety of one's being), how best to talk about it, and, most crucially, how to avoid excluding wine from the rest of one's emotional and spiritual lives.

I bring fundamental assumptions and predispositions to every bottle of wine that I drink, just as we all do, and yet these are seldom isolated, examined, or understood. We are none of us objective arrays of sensors clasping stemware; we are, rather, intricate networks of tastes and temperaments constructed over the course of lifetimes. Wine professionals have been buffeted with derision about our supposed expertise and objectivity, and we have trouble fighting back because we are defending false gods. We are not objective. And this "expertise" word they hurl at us? Every great wine soul I have known is someone who is ever a student and always on a quest. Is it expertise we seek? Of course not; it is only to remember what we've learned along the way and who we have become as we took it all in.

Because I insist that wine belongs inextricably in our lives, as do all other forms of beauty, I don't create zones where it is permitted or forbidden to live. As I have grown more pensive over time, wine enters my pensiveness. And this confers a delicious freedom, to be able to see wine meditatively. Engaged in all the viscera and substance of living, striving or dreaming, passionate or calm, there is no place from which wine *must* be excluded. It lives in the thrill and the reverie both. And all of the deepest truths I have gleaned about wine have come when I approached it indirectly, in moments when I was absorbed in something else entirely and wine peeped up—"I'm here, too." So you are, old friend!

The more meditative sections toward this book's conclusion explain how deeply and wonderfully you can hold wine in your heart when you have not insisted, *This is where it belongs and this is where it doesn't belong.* If you love wine, it belongs everywhere, and when you love the world, it lives in the world that you love.

The writer Pam Houston has something she calls "glimmers," which she uses both as noun and verb, saying, "I move through the world and I wait until something 'glimmers' at me, until something says, 'Hey writer, over here, pay attention.' [And] when I actually sit down to write and gather all the recent glimmers around me, a story does in fact emerge." If I understand her correctly, she stockpiles these glimmers until they find a permanent dwelling in a finished piece of writing. The act of recording becomes the habit of recording, and that in turn strengthens the habit of paying attention.

I bring this up because wine often appears among my own glimmers, and other glimmers that seem to have nothing ostensibly to do with wine—or "wine"—actually do. This book contains a couple chapters of my own glimmers. They're my favorites. Within them I feel like wine is in its proper proportion, among one's many beloveds, available when needed, a good friend who needn't shove everybody else out of the tent.

There are two interlocking chapters wherein I take (or attempt to take) two approaches to wine as far as they can go—in one case, to tell the entire story of the day that brought the drinker to the glass, and in the other case to describe the hero trying to obliterate himself so as to be a pure transmitter of the wine. In a certain sense these attempts don't fulfill their ostensible purposes, yet the failure actually gestates a greater insight, inching toward a lovelier question.

I am uneasily aware that all this can start to be like spun sugar, all that sweetness collecting into something that only looks like substance yet melts away. I got annoyed with myself at one point. I decided to reduce everything I could out of wine, and my conceits about wine, to see if anything would hold up —if anything would be irreducible. The result was surprising.

There are other ruminations and appreciations, but there is one great crux, one perfect summation of this book's essence, and you'll find it in the chapter "Serving the Thirsty Ghost," because—and I swear I don't intend the pun—wine lives among the spirits. Nothing that's ever entered my mind has been more forceful and mysterious than to realize that I had a new companion, who had come to me unbidden: the future ghost of me, who arrived at just the moment when I knew, viscerally, that I wouldn't always be here. What does it mean for this ghost to taste wine with me? What can I say about experiencing beauty with him behind my eyes? Why does this seem to be more crucially true than anything in my earlier life?

No one seems to have written about this — perhaps because our avenues to deep joy in wine are sometimes elliptical, and always emotional, and we're shy about our feelings. And being bashful, many of us have a kind of secret life with wine because we're shy about letting anyone see. I know this because many of you have said this to me.

Be comforted. Wine is big and often inscrutable, but your arms are large enough to encompass it.

1

THAT FIRST BOTTLE

All of us have *that first bottle*. It isn't the same first bottle, but it's the one that draws the curtain and shows us a new and different world. It's a superbly inarticulate shock that something can taste so inexplicable. *Hmmm . . . what? Uh . . . nah . . . wow! Here's something I didn't know about the world.*

I witnessed this effect recently while hosting a friend for dinner. He is a professor of musicology whom I'll call Clive, and he is every bit as cultured as his occupation would suggest. He has cultivated and accumulated expertise in a realm of aesthetics. Such interest as he may have had in wine, however, was tangential. He enjoyed wine but didn't pursue it as a hobby.

As I had thought about what to serve Clive for dinner, I decided to accompany the dishes with wine that would be excellent and would suit the food but that would not be the center of attention (as so often happens when you accept an invitation from wine people). With the first sip of the first wine, a young good Riesling from Andreas Adam on the Mosel, Clive's attention was momentarily claimed in its entirety.

"Oh my, this is good," he exclaimed. "I've never had a wine like this."

I began to form a theory, watching his captivation. I decided to test it by opening a truly exceptional wine and seeing how — or if — he would be similarly roused. It was a 2002 Hermannshöhle Spätlese from Dönnhoff, a wizard of Riesling, from his best vineyard. If there are iconic wines, this is surely among them, and anyone who has had this wine will recognize it as stellar—as, I'm happy to say, did Clive. As he drank it, it was obvious that a wine moment was taking place.

You may be like Clive. Wine is some abstruse thing. You hear people say it is interesting, but you haven't had your big wine moment. If this describes you, let me assure you of one thing: if and when you are lucky enough to have a big wine moment, you will never see it coming. Wine moments like these come along unplanned, and usually by accident.

I lucked into "that bottle" myself. I bought it at a supermarket—in Germany, where I was living at the time (and trying to suss out what on earth I planned to make of my life)—because the label said "Riesling" and I was curious about this grape I had read about but never tasted. The wine was from the giant Mosel co-op (hence its place on the supermarket shelf), and it was a 1971 Dhroner Roterd Riesling Kabinett. At that point most of what I drank was driven by fruitiness or floral aromas, but here was a wine swollen with flavor but without any fruit I could taste. There was just some weird uncanny taste of rock dust and petrichor, the smell of the air when it starts raining. All I could do was wrinkle my face as I thought, *How in the world does anything taste like this?*

When that first bottle happened to me, I was still ignorant, not even a fledgling. I was unprepared. I hadn't supposed such a thing could happen. It was only later that I started to read about wine, propelled into the urgency of learning because of *that* bottle and my growing desire for a map to bottles like that. I'd learn whatever I needed to learn so I'd know what to look for.

I think when we drink a remarkable wine, a single direct filament connects that wine to us. Even if we're gregarious and we drink most of our wine socially, at the very moment it enters us we also enter it, and we enter a thing that is strictly the two of us. How can it be otherwise? It hardly matters whether the wine is drunk in the company of others; there's a moment when *that* wine is inside *my* body, and it's *my* mind that's being charged and *my* emotions being engaged. It may happen to ten people collectively, but it's happening to each of the ten uniquely. A taste of wine can engender a numinous dialogue between a single self and all of existence.

But only good wine does this, or at least a wine that's good enough for me not to dismiss it. It doesn't have to be great. If it is, then the dialogue is important or even profound. But any worthy wine that assumes one's attention, if only for the slightest of moments, has the force of a message. Ordinary pleasure is subsumed into an odd sense of something being said to us.

Some people are comfortable making objects of wine. It becomes a form of entertainment for which they are spectators. It isn't wrong, but it's a wasted opportunity, because wine grows richer to the extent we see it as a form of life with which we engage as fellow beings. I often feel we've placed wine in a kind of ghetto behind a tall fence, making it a "thing" someone "does" rather than a companion that walks with us.

If wine had turned out to be merely sensual, I think for me its joys would have been transitory. I'd have done "the wine thing" for a certain number of years and gone on to something else. What continued to drive me, and what drives many of us, is curiosity, pleasure in surprise, and those elusive but incandescent moments of meaning—the sense that some truth, normally obscure, is being revealed.

So I kept pushing forward, until I started to sense a greater congruence between what I was tasting and who I was, tasting. And then it was like a prong clicking neatly into a sprocket. Wine suddenly wouldn't stay behind the fence. It insisted on roaming through the world of other beautiful beings, and there was hardly a corner of my life it didn't visit.

Can this possibly take place before one attains a certain age? I wonder. Perhaps there's indeed a moment and a place where beauty and mortality intersect. Perhaps if a man reaches that point, beauty is no longer a thing he looks at from a position of remove, but instead it is a being that he absorbs into his very cells. Wine has a curious way of constantly renewing your curiosity, but even that might not have sufficed for a lifetime of joy. It is the invitation wine offers, access to a vivid sort of beauty, that keeps us thirsting. Now I find myself looking at many things of beauty in the same way, and they all have keys to one another's houses. Each of them lives within all of them.

I didn't know any of this when I first went exploring, during those Wanderjahren in Germany when I was in my twenties. I needed to know the ways to other mind-bending bottles like that '71 Dhroner, but otherwise I just hoped to be competent. I'd learn what I had to learn to recapture that experience.

I found a self-published little chapbook—I wish I still had it, or at least recalled the author's name—that was sold at the McGraw Kasern army newsstand in Munich (where I bought my copies of *Crawdaddy* and *Rolling Stone*), and this little book gave the basics, and also contained lists of the better vineyards in the major regions. The metamessage was, vineyards were important. Learn the best ones and you'll find the best wines. This was no help at all when I returned to the supermarkets that sold me the plonk I'd been drinking. Clearly I needed to upgrade my sources.

At the same time I'd found an early edition of the Hugh Johnson *World Atlas of Wine*, which offered both a ton of good hard data and the reassurance of confirming that my aha moment was more than a fluke. My god, was I lucky. Who is so lucky these days? My formative influence was a good writer, a civilized and knowledgeable fellow, and someone who not only permitted but *encouraged* emotional responses to wine. My "moment" with that bottle—I want to write That Bottle —wasn't as extraordinary as I'd feared. Wine had the power to move a person.

Once in a while I've said that wine rescued me, and it's true, because I don't know what else I'd have done for a living. But wine was more than a way to a vocation. It was a curiously beckoning threshold, to something that felt like home. I knew; my heart was meant for this. I knew; I could draw from the best of me. I knew; I could be ever-fascinated and ever-grateful. (I could maybe even . . . make a living. Maybe. I knew I wanted to, *had* to, though I didn't remotely know how. That would come later.)

I see now that each time I drank good wine I assumed it was exactly as alive as I was. Was this some sort of quirk of mine? It didn't feel that way. It was nothing I arrived at. I assumed it with no conscious thought at all: a glass of wine has a life just as a poem does, or a piece of music, or even a good joke. I don't elevate it by bestowing upon it all the sublime glory of my miraculous humanity. Nor does it elevate me. The little message from the universe it delivers is a reminder and an affirmation. If the message is singularly beautiful, then I am singularly roused, and being roused, I may access a state of sublimity, at least a little. It's tempting to suppose the wine contains or entails the sublimity I feel, but this I cannot know. I rather think the wine simply brings a message: that there is a vast universe, an infinitude of things existing, and only one of them is me. The rest of them are not me and have almost nothing to do with me. And so, if the extent of a wine's message is to remind me to be able to absorb the world and be ready to look into it openly and with humility, that's as much as can be asked. If the wine is arrestingly or hauntingly beautiful, that is a gift, one I did nothing to earn and can only accept.

These days I feel more introspective than I did in my beginnings with wine. Among its many lessons is a delicate admonition: learn to relax. My wife and I live near Harvard University's Arnold Arboretum, and, it being Harvard's, it's an orderly, sylvan, and civilized place. Except for two parts, one a tall hill that entails a bit of a clamber and the other a sweet little place I'll tell you about now. Just off a paved path there's a little dirt path along a hidden creek, and in about ten steps you're really all by yourself. It's no great shakes and it doesn't go for long, but when you come to the small wooden bridge you can pause and listen to the splishing of the creek, and maybe see a turtle if you're lucky. I love it because it's so small and lost and forgotten, and the water sounds like someone singing who's shy about her voice.

I love tiny hidden things. I want to be one. I want to do just one thing but do it purely and do it when no one's watching. My professional persona is a thing I portray, a kind of enactment that comes from me but isn't me. And yet it helps me sell wine and be the growers' champion, as I want to be. I try, fitfully and rarely with success, to integrate these two men, but I can't help it: I feel more real when I'm sitting alone writing, such as right now, than when I'm being whatever personage the occasion asks me to be. I did a trade seminar one year in San Francisco, and I'd been reading William Stafford's poems, so I decided to read one to the crowd before we started tasting. They humored me, and the poem wasn't very long. And I felt like a fool, of course, but even as I cringed inside, I was glad I did it. Turn your cell phones off but your souls on, good folk.

One simply doesn't talk about wine this way with other wine lovers, you see. Or at least I rarely do. We can draw near this mystical aspect of wine, but as we do, our common language seems to falter. This makes sense; after all, when does a single wine move different drinkers in the same way? I'll tell you what I mean.

Much of wine's allure, the elements that keep you charged for a whole lifetime, relates to what the psychologist Abraham Maslow called the "peak experience." This has many definitions, depending on your source material, and even Maslow himself had more than one. But all of them relate to a sense of enormous *meaning*, something that wasn't exactly pleasure but brought pleasure with it, something that wasn't joy but encompassed joyfulness, but above all, something that carried an odd force of truth, as if this condition of wonder and affirmation were authentic while ordinary consciousness was in fact a distortion. Everyone who's ever described these experiences, whether they use Maslow's term or one among many other terms, has remarked on the curious conviction that a pure, vast reality is being apprehended.

Certain wines, at certain moments, can have this effect on us. One cannot anticipate these experiences, nor summon them. They arrive, if at all, to those who are available and prepared. Nor is there a single template for such "preparation," though in my case it may have to do with my assumption that beauty is meaningful. Yet I have stood before the most sublime vistas and no peak experiences were in the vicinity. There's no recipe; you can't just cook them up.

Recently I popped into the Slanted Door restaurant in San Francisco, to sit at the bar and have a few oysters and a glass of wine. I sell them wine, and they recognized me, which was touching and made me feel bashful. The bar was full, but they managed to find a chair and sat me at the end. I was softened by their kindness, and happy to be alone, and hungry for those oysters. Presently they arrived, and I assembled glasses of three different wines to survey and contrast compatibilities. Various staff members came by to say hello. Some of them hugged me. The oysters were briny and sweet. The wines were lovely. I looked around me, at the women working the hostess stand, at the guys shucking oysters, at the tourists and through the door to the water and the gulls outside. Quite abruptly, every single thing was beautiful. I suddenly understood what Yeats meant when he wrote, "My body of a sudden blazed; / And twenty minutes more or less / It seemed, so great my happiness, / That I was blessed, and could bless."

These moments of meaning, it seems, can be chemically induced, by LSD or mescaline or Ecstasy, and we know the areas of the brain that are stimulated (or suppressed) to bring them about. That would seem to cheapen it—satori brought to you by pharmacology. (Two sides to every satori, I suppose.) And yet I wonder. Let us suppose that we do know what cerebral neurochemical chain reaction makes us surmise that existence is meaningful and beautiful. This compels the question, why should this be there at all? Everything in the brain seems to have a job to do or a purpose to serve, so why is evolution concerned with humans feeling that life is astonishing and real? In other words, what evolutionary purpose is being served by this "mystical" capacity? It seems reasonable to suppose it belongs there. Or it seems at least more reasonable than to suppose it's there accidentally.

None of this means you give away your earthly possessions and build a yurt in Big Sur somewhere. It means, when such impulses visit you, you don't repel or subdue them. Feel as weird as you like, but let them in. If I can have a peak experience eating oysters by myself in a place where the people seem fond of me, then you can have one at the ballgame, or behind the wheel, or repairing a furnace.

Lately I've been able to score some old German Rieslings. I love those wines like you wouldn't believe. It's been absolute bliss to drink them, but until a recent evening I'd had no peak experiences with them—just all kinds of fun.

I was pulling bottles from cases to see what I'd open, my wife and I having decided that the holiday season was a good time to indulge. The first bottle I grasped had about four inches of ullage, thanks to a leaky cork. This was a 1953 Rauenthaler Gehrn Auslese (a special selection of overripe bunches of grapes, from which a rich sweet wine is usually made) from the Staatsdomain, my birth year: too bad! It had to be opened immediately, yet it wouldn't be enough wine, so much having been lost. Its neighbor was a 1966 Auslese, from Thörnicher Ritsch, from a grower named Johann Geiben, who I'm sure has since shut his doors. We needed them both—gotta have enough wine!

The '53 was the color of Pedro Ximénez Sherry, and though the wine had some burnt caramel notes, it was wonderfully malty and pure. Still rather sweet, and under any other circumstances it would have been sipped with all due worshipfulness. But that '66 was just poured, and soon all thoughts of the '53 vanished. For when we took our first sip of that second Auslese, I knew we were in for it.

I hardly write tasting notes anymore. Either I want to write nothing or I want to write pages and pages, just narrating the process of being flung out into the dust. Looked at as wine qua wine, this '66 was perfect; pale gold, pale nuttiness, still showing some of its baby flavors of herbs and shady green teas. It was even still slatey—it grew on slate—with a wet-cereal sweetness, and its minerality wouldn't let up, as if it entailed a matcha powder strained through primary slate, and as always with old Riesling it did its Benjamin Button act, getting fresher and springier in the glass until finally it was almost limpid, calmly breathing its vetiver and wet straw over us.

The night was miserable; cold driving rain seeming to blow horizontally under the streetlights. Still I went outside to drink that Riesling in the cold fresh air. I stood there under my little porch roof, under the relentless rain, and though the night was brutal the wine was a baby cooing its idiot heart out. When I came inside my mind was vibrating with image-stories I couldn't write down quickly enough. They had to do with funerals and with newborns, with memorial services where a baby was gurgling with laughter under her mobile in the corner and with all that incomprehensible expanse of time on either side of our little lives. What I produced that night was not your average tasting note—but then again, this was not your average wine.

These aren't, alas, the wines I can find for my customers—old wines are rare, and when you find them it's only a bottle here or a bottle there. But many of the wines I offer will become wines like these, assuming one has good storage and a lot of patience. If I look for what I call wines of soul, that doesn't mean "soul" comes in a beaker and can be added to the wine. But it will not appear at all if it finds a wine inhospitable, and so

I look for wines where soul might find a perch. Those elements, those prerequisites (we might say), are not as nebulous as one might suspect, and I describe them explicitly in the pages ahead. My thirsts as a wine lover—for soul, companionability, authenticity—inform my choices as a wine merchant, and the larger value of what I seek to do is not only to please your senses but to enrich your lives.

2

TURNOVER! TURNOVER! TURNOVER!

My wine moment occurred in Europe, as I have written. I couldn't get the job I wanted at *New Musical Express* and I was tiring of the rock-musician-in-a-band life, the cigarette smoke, the noise, the schlepping around of amps and drums, so I did bits and pieces of things. I gave guitar lessons, I worked at Germany's first-ever McDonald's—where, I am proud to report, I was fired after six hideous weeks—I worked in the warehouse of a company that made milking machines (their motto was "We take care of the cow!"), and eventually I got a job as a civilian component of the Defense Department, which sounds terribly hoity-toity until I tell you what it entailed: I cleaned rooms in an army hotel. If I ever have to create a dating-site profile again, I'll be sure to trumpet "outstanding housework skills, especially toilets!"

The job was in some ways ideal. The hours were regular, and while the pay was pathetic, my wife's and my needs were very few. We didn't have a car, we didn't have a TV, we didn't have a telephone, we walked to work and lived in a fully furnished apartment whose rent included utilities and was very small. So we had a pittance of income, but almost all of it was disposable. And with generous government bennies, like ample vacation time, we had every reason to go exploring, once wine had us in its toothy grip.

This was the late '70s—simpler times. The wine books I

read talked about vineyards, wine estates, all the things that made wine what it was. So when we set out on our wine adventures, we first went to the places from which great wine was said to originate. I was looking for wines from certain vineyards, and when I made it to the villages to which they belonged, I saw signs everywhere for small growers selling their wines directly to the public.

Not all the growers were good. Luckily, I seemed to be able to discern, and we developed a sort of de facto list of favorites to whom we went repeatedly. The larger point is this: my earliest imprinting, the experiences that formed my wine template, were inextricably connected to vineyards and families. This was certainly true in Germany, and it was also true in Alsace, Burgundy, the Loire, and not true in Bordeaux, a region by which I was perplexed and nonplussed. Why was it so aloof and unwelcoming?

Of course I grew aware of the existence of large-scale "industrial" wine. Indeed, I was asked to write about the gigantic central cooperative in the Baden region, at the time the world's third largest winery, and when I began to try to get work within the German wine trade, it was the big schlockmeisters who answered my ad. (One interview concluded with the guy pounding his fist on the table and shouting, "It's about *Umsatz! Umsatz! Umsatz!*"—Turnover! Turnover! Turnover!—while my face went ashen and the ashtrays rattled.)

My wife wanted to return to the States and I wanted to stay married, and so I somewhat reluctantly followed her. My first job in the "beverage industry" was working wholesale for a midsized distributor, who sent me into all the accounts we had either never called on or been thrown out of. But working around the army had helped; I had learned to get along with all kinds of people, and I was a wine naïf and not a slick sales dude, and I kind of liked calling on the unmapped and perilous accounts. Here there be dragons, and all that; it was fun.

In the early days of my employ, no one paid me much heed

except to peer over every now and again to see whether I'd been fired yet. I could sell what I liked. I took out the wines I was interested in and made some improbable headway. Eventually I became a strange fixture, this abnormal wine guy who'd lived in Germany but who was actually writing business, and as my stature grew my territory changed and I had more consequential accounts.

This isn't merely my fascinating picaresque tale of triumph over all who had doubted me—I doubted myself, if it came to that—but a struggle began to enter the picture. As I became a more mainstream sales rep, I needed to "make numbers" and fulfill quotas, and much of what makes distributors functional is satisfying their key suppliers, who provide the revenue by which they survive. This meant I needed to extol the virtues of a lot of mundane, commercial, industrial wine. Now, I wasn't so special back then and I'm still not. This is what most wholesale reps do: make numbers on the wines their company needs to sell, and in their spare time—if they have any—they get to sell the wines they themselves prefer.

I adored a kind of wine that wasn't light and crisp (our British friends call them cheap and cheerful) and wasn't big and bold; it was somewhere in between, and its outlines didn't matter. The way it *tasted* mattered. Yet in the trade there's a regrettable tendency to sell cheap stuff because it's cheap and monumental stuff because there's a geek drinker who grasps at greatness and for whom only the best will do, and lost in all this polarization are those wines in between, which simply happen to taste delicious.

I tried to be good at the work. I did the job and made the numbers. But something started siphoning the juice from my soul. It wasn't the existence of silly commercial wine, but instead it was the cynicism and pretension of using the lingo and the sensibilities of (let's agree to call them) "fine" wines in order to sell the other stuff. It devalued every aspect of my formative experience, asserting the absence of any line between what

I knew to be *valid* wines and these other items, which I began to call "beverages containing wine."

So what? So this: corruption of language encourages corruption of thought, and if the language of fine wine could be appropriated to describe (and sell) banal commercial wine, then that language was stripped of its value. And that language is all we have! I was also annoyed at the underlying contempt for wine "romanticism" such as mine, as its salespeople thieved its lingo to sell their beverages as though that language were as worthless as the twee idealism it indicated.

It grew clear that my days as a wholesale rep were numbered. I wasn't at all too haughty to sell wines I didn't like. But it was ever more awkward to have to extol the virtues of an entire genre of "wine" that I didn't believe in.

I am no doubt angrier than most wine people about this ostensibly matter-of-fact reality, I admit. The world of small-batch family estate wines rolls on, doing quite well for itself, it would seem. Yet its values, I think, are in ceaseless peril, unless they are explained and defended. They are primary and basic, so much so that we sometimes lose track of them. We take them as given. Yet they are not.

Consider this: in my work as an importer of small-grower Champagnes, I have helped make these wines conspicuous, and from all appearances it has been a great success. As indeed it has; most of my growers have run out of wine to supply me, and everyone is giddy. And yet—the entire share of the U.S. market for this Champagne category hovers around 5 percent. The biggest three "brands" dominate, with nearly two-thirds of all American sales. My largest grower bottles in an entire year what the biggest Champagne house has bottled by about 2 p.m. on January 2. David's a resolute and creative fighter, but sometimes Goliath just stomps on his head. Vigilance is key, and we small-batch merchants can't assume we'll prevail just because we're so adorable.

Indeed, the truly spurious "romance" is what's used to market big industrial wines rather than small-batch wines from actual vineyards and people, not the folks in corporate boardrooms clutching spreadsheets but people back from a morning in the vineyards with muddy boots and gunk under their nails. It's dangerously easy to conclude that all wine romance is bogus because the most conspicuous wine romance is indeed bogus. It's harder to appreciate the authentic and the reasons it matters.

I came to know that I would survive in the wine business only if I could champion that which I truly loved and believed in. If you have ever worked in sales, you will agree that selling involves manipulating, and manipulating almost always entails . . . let's say, shading the truth. It's not that my soul is so delicate. Part of me liked to make the sale. But it was hollow, and I was a man in disguise, and I knew I'd be found out. I needed to be able to sell wines I knew were worth drinking, and to say why.

What really makes a wine worth drinking? Why should we care? For my more wine-savvy readers, this could seem remedial, because we have internalized it so deeply. But the average wine consumer, who isn't obsessed (yet!) but who is interested enough to find herself reading this book, could maybe make use of a statement of basic values before we dive deeper into the emotional and spiritual gifts of great wine.

3

WHAT MAKES A WINE
WORTH DRINKING?

What a silly, boneheaded question, right? It's one of those self-evident, "Why is there air?" sorts of questions that people use to produce noise (or copy) masquerading as substance.

Or is it?

The apparent answer, of course, is that a wine is worth drinking if you like it, if it gives you pleasure. But the truth is more complex than that. I am not insisting you drink a wine you don't like. You have nothing to prove to me, or to anyone. But there are reasons for choosing among types of things, and what you "like" is not as simple as it seems.

Inasmuch as a Triscuit, that little quotidian cracker, has been exquisitely designed and manipulated to have an aftertaste that will get you to *eat another Triscuit,* it is clear that commercial wines can be similarly designed and manipulated by experts who know your taste better than you do. If a wine has been formed to access your reptilian or infantile pleasure centers by some swami who's trained to hypnotize an unaware subject, would you insist that such a wine is worth drinking? (The wine writer Stuart Pigott calls this effect—brilliantly—"fluffy-white-bunny taste.")

The key word, of course, is "worth." And to talk about worth, you have to make value judgments. So I'll make mine, and you'll see if you agree.

To start, you should know—in addition to all the other things I've told you about myself—that I am the product of a sweet and loving and almost comically stereotypical Jewish mother, whom I could withstand only by learning to identify and ultimately resist the guilt trip. It entailed a certain amount of collateral damage, as my wife will be glad to tell you, because I evolved a rhinoceros hide that was damnably hard to dissolve later on, when I actually needed to let other people affect me. But it had a positive side: it made me extra-sensitive to manipulations in all forms and gave me a better chance against them.

The more you are impervious to manipulation, the more you are free. That doesn't mean I can stop at one Triscuit. I wish I could! But it does mean, as I plunge my gormless greedy hand into the box, that I've consciously chosen to be manipulated and can consciously choose not to be by avoiding, among other things, Triscuits.

One year I had a condo to sell, and it was illuminating to talk with the realtor and learn the many ways potential buyers can be subliminally manipulated, to the point of making pumpkin pie on the day of an open house so that your place has an inviting aroma. Luckily, I sold the place before having to list it, but I was uneasy with the whole business of staging and am glad I didn't have to resort to it.

Mind you, manipulation isn't inherently evil, but I have serious reservations about its stealthy and dishonest forms. All viniculture is manipulation; wine doesn't actually make itself, except in certain people's romantic notions (the marketing of which is its own form of manipulation). But a useful dichotomy exists: one either preserves inherent flavor, or one adds flavor that wasn't already there and couldn't have been there.

A typical commercial wine begins with grapes with little taste of their own other than generic grape flavor. If you ferment them as they are, you get a bland wine. So your winemaking Svengali starts by adding yeasts and enzymes to the juice to create "attractive" aromas. (Enter the cute little bunny.) You then set about manipulating the alcohol and texture of the wine, which marketing types refer to as "mouthfeel," by various externally derived means. (Too much alcohol can seem "jammy," even to drinkers who like that kind of thing, so most manipulations of alcohol involve reducing it to find a so-called sweet spot where your toes will curl and the critics will sigh as they award their scores.) You can also add flavor by using oak, or its semblance, and you can ramp up the yummy factor by adjusting or adding residual sugar. This is how the bunny gets its fluff.

The final "wine" is little more than a *device*, a thing by which a consumer is seduced, a peek at a cleavage of silicone. It has been designed to appeal to you and, even worse, to leave you blissfully unaware. It cannot address your intelligence or discernment or imagination or taste. It cannot address *you* at all. It whispers to you subliminally. And the next thing you know, you're drinking this product and calling it wine.

Have you ever manipulated someone, in your professional or personal life? How did you feel afterward about the person or people you manipulated? The brutal, honest answer is that you held them in contempt. You duped them, the simple fools. So ask yourself this: do the people who fashion all these wines to appeal to the masses do it because they respect the masses? As if! You are just a unit that responds predictably to stimuli they have learned how to engineer.

I think you should rebel. Unless, of course, you're content to be a consumer unit who submits to having your infantile pleasure centers diddled. In that case, at least surrender knowingly.

Put it this way. If I were a poet and I gave readings, I would hope that my audience found the poems interesting and maybe even moving. If I were a good reader, I could juice the poems a little, read them theatrically. I could sequence the poems so that I captured my audience early on and encouraged them to follow the flow. All of this is manipulation, but none of it is objectionable. Indeed, the audience is hoping to be moved, to fall under a spell. But what if I played somber music? What if I played it below the audible threshold but it still registered with the audience? What if I showed pictures on a screen behind me, of sad puppies or limbless children or rainbows and waterfalls? I'd be a poet who didn't trust his poems. Don't you ever feel irritated by movies where the big swollen music arrives at some Big Moment just so you'll know exactly how you're intended to feel? All I know in those moments is that a shitty filmmaker doesn't trust that the unadorned material is enough to *make* people feel. Or that he needs so badly to have power over us that he'll take any shortcut he can find.

So if I'm that kind of winemaker, I need the same power over you, because I want to sell a heaving mass of wine, and I will do anything necessary to guarantee those sales. And if that means I press buttons you don't even know exist, then that's what it means. I need the business. I have shareholders to answer to, or debt to service, or I'm just good at aesthetic propaganda and I like to strut. You don't even exist, except as a lemming to which a sale is attached.

And so I argue that such wines are *not* worth drinking, no matter that people like them or can be induced to suppose they do.

What makes a wine worth drinking is that it is honest and authentic. That and nothing more.

Once we are confident that a wine is true, we can make all kinds of judgments and discernments and maybe discover that some wines are more worth drinking than others, according to our tastes or frames of reference or systems of values. With all the sad commercial dross swept away, the real discussion can begin. But it all begins with this simple question: what makes a wine honest and authentic?

It tastes of what it is. And what it is involves what ground it grew in, where it came from, what weather it ripened in, who made it and how. Note that these are not value-weighted qualities. Such a wine could be, hypothetically, a Silvaner grown on clay in a warmish region in a hot vintage, made by an average grower who didn't really adapt to the particulars of the harvest. It might be, in short, an ordinary or even dull wine. But. It is *valid* wine, and it is still more worth drinking than any commercial item even if the popular wine is more superficially attractive. Please don't misconstrue here; I am not mounting an argument in favor of dull wines. I am saying that at the start of this discussion, quality doesn't matter. It will matter hugely later on, but not yet. What matters now is that we agree about what makes wines honest and authentic. These are the broad strokes, which need to be in place before we can consider the finer points.

So "it tastes of what it is." Meaning what, exactly?

First, what it is is discernible. Nothing obtrudes upon it or obscures it. You can recognize it as *that* sort of wine. It is Bandol, or Chianti, or Vouvray or Finger Lakes Riesling or Rioja, but whatever it is, we can taste what it is. In other words, the wine is distinctive. It may be grossly distinctive—a "southern Rhône," perhaps—or finely distinctive ("this just *has* to be Rayas"), but in any case it is recognizable.

Part of why you can recognize such a wine is that its basic nature is clear, because it hasn't been veneered with oak or other additives. That doesn't mean "no oak." It means oak hasn't obliterated the wine's character.

What-it-is may mean varietal identity, soil identity, or both. That said, I have more trust in soil than I do in variety. There's a winery in Austria whose wines all smell like Scheurebe, a white wine grape grown primarily in that country and in Germany; even the Grüner Veltliners smell like Scheu. It's said to be some enzyme the vintner uses. Certain varietal markers are easy to imitate, so a wine that smells like Sauvignon Blanc is less interesting to me than a wine that smells like Pouilly-Fumé, because the latter is more a question of soil and of the singularity of place.

Soil identity makes itself known throughout the world of wine. Basalt in the Pfalz, slate on the Mosel, primary rock in the

Nahe and Wachau, Caillou in Châteauneuf, limestone in Burgundy and granite in Beaujolais, tufa in Touraine, Kimmeridgian clay in Chablis, belemnite chalk in Champagne . . . the list goes on. And even where strict soil expression isn't blatant, we can often infer it. If a wine smells like Nebbiolo, it's probably Piedmontese, because Nebbiolo hardly grows elsewhere, which is because it prefers the soils and environments of Piedmont to those of any other place.

Soil is a better locator than grape, and we want wines to be located because we want all things, *including ourselves,* to be located. Each thing and being belongs someplace. Home is what we start from and return to. The more specific the origin, the more interesting the wine. And not only wine. Darjeeling tea is interesting because it comes from a particular place in the hills of northern India. Its character is born of that place. We can go even deeper and select from among a range of producers, microclimates, and even terroirs, and we can select among various pluckings both in different seasons and within each one. Even vintages vary, as the weather varies so high up and close to the Himalayas. A bag of Twinings English Breakfast consisting of dust and fannings from a slew of different teas may be useful at times, but it is not merely inferior to the estate Darjeeling, it is a different order of being. One thing is particular and the other is generic.

We may consume the generic, but we don't pay attention to it. Only the particular warrants our attention. If a wine does not cause us to notice it, why are we drinking it?

A wine is worth drinking when it communicates its singular distinctive being. That is, it is *honest and authentic.* That is what makes it valid.

Everything matters to a valid wine, but we need to assign an order of salience among these things. My own priorities are soil (content and structure), exposure, microclimate, mesoclimate, and human influence. Others may dispute these priorities, and often have, so here's why I say what I do.

I think of the hands on a clock. The hour hand moves so slowly we cannot see it move and know of its having moved only if we look away and then back. The hour hand symbolizes the soil, because it changes extremely slowly and sometimes barely at all. (I am aware of changes brought about by humans and the chemical inputs we sometimes use, but this is better addressed when we talk about all human influences.)

The minute hand moves more quickly but is also hard to discern. I liken it to the human influence, which may shift according to someone's whims and caprices or may be grounded in deeply held principles. Or both. It changes in a fundamental way only when proprietorship changes, as between generations. And sometimes even then it hardly changes.

The second hand is the one we can see flick along, and this represents the weather, which changes ceaselessly, moment by moment. Whatever the prevailing mesoclimate may be, any given year is full of surprises.

Soil is the basis. Soil writes the text. Soil *is* the text. The human is the reader of the text. And the weather is the costume worn by the human who reads the text.

If soil is primary, as I argue, then it follows that the most honest and authentic wines are those in which its primacy is apparent and its influence may be tasted. Please don't assume this means mineral flavors are paramount. They may well be, but if so it's for rather different reasons. Soil can just as easily express itself by iterations of fruity or herbal or flowery notes. Grüner Veltliner from a primary-rock Grand Cru will certainly taste ferrous and rocky, but it will also taste like vetiver (a root), like boxwood (a leaf), and like rhubarb or strawberries. And it could well be scented of irises. Each of these is a marker of terroir born of soil.

When a wine's flavor is *inherent,* it is expressing something about its home. We needn't have words for it; all we need is to look on. A wine's home is layered; there's its particular place (say the great Wehlener Sonnenuhr), its general place (the fjord-like Mosel Valley and the Devonian slate of its vineyards), its more general place (northern Europe and its quality of daylight and climate), and its final place (the earth itself). A great wine writes a text of the entire world, radiating out from the specific to the general. *This is where I live, and this is where* we *live.* Perhaps you pause for a moment, as the wine makes you more human. Because it does.

When a wine's flavor is inherent, the person who makes it is dealing with flavors he didn't create. If it's a small family domain, passed along through generations, the people are also inherent, deeply at home in their little nook of the world. Vine and human alike are at home, and unified. Their unity helps make a wine authentic. When someone works to make a beautiful thing that also expresses the inchoate truth of its identity, that person is serving the cause of existence itself. We are not only grateful *we* exist, we are grateful things exist — we are grateful *existence* exists. All because the grapes that person grows seem to give almost eerily imprinted flavors to his or her wines. (One grower once said to me, "They aren't only my wines, they're *their* wines," as he spread his arms toward his vineyards.) I find this to be fundamentally good. Because it begins with someone keenly aware of the existence of something as real as she herself is. "Those flavors are *there,* and their existence is as crucial as my own. So I am not here in order to *make* flavor. I don't have to and wouldn't want to; I have this wordless gift from the soil. What I want to do is love it, tend it carefully and competently, and see that it sings."

Thus do vintners appreciate and celebrate the world. Thus may we do the same.

And it is a powerful marker of soul, both for them as doers and for us as onlookers. "Soul" will be talked about in the pages to come, but for now let me propose it as a confluence of terroir, family, and artisanality that gives a wine a sense of existential life. That elevates it from a mere thing to an actual being, that can speak to our own souls.

These, then, are the prerequisites, the things we want to establish before we address the question of "how the wine tastes." Put it this way: if you have a hamburger place nearby and the proprietors bake their own organic bread and use local grass-ranged beef, what do you do if the burger isn't good? What, particularly, do you do if there's a conventional commercial place down the street that has really good burgers? The standard answer is, you go where the food tastes better. You shouldn't sacrifice flavor just to do the "right" thing. But this isn't my answer. I wouldn't go to *either* place. I'd keep looking until I found a place that does the "right" thing *and* knows how to cook a burger. I'd travel farther if I had to.

Of course, I sympathize with the assertion that we should drink what we like; as long as it's good, then what does it matter who made it or how? To which I would reply, if you were deciding between two pairs of sneakers, and both of them fit and were comfortable, and they cost about the same, but one pair was made in a factory in China (and who knows how the workers were treated?) and the other was made in a little sneaker operation a few miles away—what then?

My point is, we make political choices all the time in the marketplace. We get to make one here, as we choose what kinds of wines to include in our lives. You don't have to make the same one I would make, but you're disingenuous if you try to lay a populist guilt trip on me for drawing these lines. The lines are there—I didn't put them there. And you get to have a tiny influence over the kind of world you prefer to live in. So make your choice and dance.

Having done so—and having made just the very choice I asked you to make, naturally—it's time to open a bottle and drink. And, most crucially, it's time to *respond*.

How could we not respond? you ask. I'll tell you how. We fail to respond to the extent that we fail to pay attention.

To be sure, some wines demand less attention than others—not because such wines are unworthy, but because they don't clamor. They don't yell as they express themselves. Maybe they're just tasty and fun, tactful companions keeping us company. But even then we've attended to all the many things that led up to *that* choice of bottle. We aren't slumming. We didn't pick something mundane, we picked something *modest*. Two very different things. In the world of authentic wines there are many everyday citizens. Everyone can't be royalty. If each wine you drink demands your full attention, what's left for everything else? And if you're always cruising among the stellar, your baseline gets so lofty that you don't perceive the stellar anymore. You are numbed and jaded by having repeated one single experience. If you have birthday sex every time, what do you do on your birthday?

For the wines that *do* reward attention, however, our mere attendance can yield a host of responses, leading to a far deeper engagement with the wine than you may have thought possible. At the moment of tasting, if I could slow it down and freeze-frame my responses, they'd take the form of these questions.

What does it taste like?

Is it a direct, candid taste, or is it an allusive, mysterious taste? Is it a simple taste or a complex taste?

How would I describe the taste to someone else?

How does the wine behave? What is its temperament? Is it demure, brash, frisky, serene, boisterous, regal?

How does the wine make me feel?

Does the wine refer to anything beyond itself? Does it evoke or suggest other things (such as music) or other states of being?

These responses aren't exactly linear; rather, they exist within an ad hoc system of concentric circles in the ways we react to wine and talk and write about it. We ourselves stand in the center of the innermost circle. The image holds true for most of us, most of the time; it's plausible. I do not refer to the various tasting protocols used by different certification organizations, most prominently the Master Sommelier. Those protocols are fine for training people to be good blind tasters (for whatever that may be worth, but let's not fuss over it again). For the rest of us, what I'm describing here isn't a system of any kind; it's a depiction of a process most of us use anyway to deepen our understanding and enjoyment of a wine.

The narrowest of the circles, the first one, is how we react immediately to the first sip. We are tasting effects for which we seek causes. "What is this, and how did it happen?" We may look at terroir, if that is our habit and our default marker. Or we may look at cellar practices—or both, of course—but in any case we're trying to taste the what, why, and how. This is especially (but not uniquely) true if we're tasting blind. This narrowest of the circles is somewhat constricting and not a lot of fun. We'd like to wriggle free of it. (It feels too much like work!)

As we arrive at the next circle, we want to give language to what we're tasting. Sometimes it's only we ourselves who wish to remember the wine. We may write impressions down to aid our memory. Sometimes we want to tell other people what we drank and how it tasted. At this point the fur flies.

Flavor is famously difficult to talk about. How would you describe the difference between, let's say, ground veal and ground beef? Between an orange and a tangerine? Most often you end up in a sort of self-referential Möbius strip of language. "The beef tastes . . . oh, I don't know, *beefier*." And yet we seem to need to try. So we start by associating the present wine flavor with other flavors that our readers or listeners will know—"It smells/tastes like berries"—and then of course we slide down the slippery slope. We don't want to seem obtuse or mundane. So we can't leave it at "berries." Now it has to be blueberries or huckleberries or elderberries. Maybe these associations are true, or true enough, but in many cases they are less about the wine than about the taster showing off his adorable brilliant palate. Thus we get into the whole "ermine eyelashes steeped in chilled mead and sprinkled with crushed cat dander" school of tasting notes.

I recognize it is useful to stretch the mental muscle as we

concentrate to find associations with other things we know. It's good to work the mind. But I think it's like walking on a treadmill: it's good exercise, but it's only the illusion of forward motion. Because even if these flavor associations are valid, we have effectively stated a kind of tautology: to say a wine smells like lemons is to say that lemons smell like lemons. Fine: what do lemons smell like? Beyond the elementary need to say *something* about a wine, this simulacrum of communication leaves much to be desired. The syllogisms this-tastes-like-that do not take us anywhere. We are still too constricted by our need to be exact and literal.

The next outer circle entails that we deconstruct a wine's structure and interpret the inferences to be drawn from it. How vivid are the different building blocks (tannin, acidity, etc.) and how elegantly are they organized? How is the wine's texture, and is it pleasing? We are beginning perhaps to *appreciate*. Sensuality hears its name being called. Up to now we've been busily trying to subdue the wine, to pin its shoulders to the mat until it surrenders its secrets. But now we glean the timorous arrival, dare I say, of pleasure.

From this point on it starts to get interesting. What we've done so far is to kick the tires and look at the engine and examine the fit and finish and where the buttons are. Now we get to see how it feels to drive the vehicle.

These new, larger orbits give us the perspective to make the wine fascinating in itself, not merely as a specimen we use to perform our cerebral strut. From here we're asking more salient questions. What can we infer about the place from which this wine hails? That is, from its macro (Old World, Burgundy) and micro (Côte du Beaune, Volnay, Caillerets) identities. By which gestures does the wine convey its origin? Perhaps we pause here, to appreciate even for a small moment that wines do tell us where they come from. Perhaps we sense that this is something meaningful. Perhaps we're happy to be part of a process that can start to feel miraculous. But even if we feel none of those things, asking the "where" question is always preferable to asking the "how" question. The "how" can usually be explained by technique and engineering. But the "where" is explained by elements of identity and feelings of home.

We start to relax when we reach this point. Instead of lunging toward the wine, we're willing to let it come to us. As it approaches we ask, what sort of personality does this wine have? Is it charming, imperious, hyperactive, pensive? What sort of texture does it offer? Is it crisp or creamy, nubby or sumptuous? What is its feeling tone? Is it contemplative, energetic, clever, profound? I find it terribly sad that such language is often debased as inauthentic, because it tells me much more about a wine than the prevailing geek-speak. And yes, of course it can be badly used; it can seem twee, it can be a fallback for tasters simply trying to impress their fellow drinkers. It needs good hands and a sense of humor, and I think it's useful to have a leavening of vulgarity as a hedge against preciousness. So the wine dances like a faery queen, and screw you if you don't agree!

The best comes last. Some wines, such as a wine called Souches Mères (which I describe fully in a later chapter), are so haunting and stirring that they bypass our entire analytical faculty and fill us with image and feeling. We glean the larger purpose of wine, and of beauty, and of life. And we sense a unity that's often oblique to our gaze. The friend who served my silly reluctant self this lovely wine had visited Giulio Moriondo, the proprietor, who was reputed to be irascible, as mavericks often are. Much to my friend's surprise, he was cordial, almost sweet. Like the maker, the wine has a lyric paradox of warm and cool tones; it's surrounded by mountains but not especially high in altitude, and like the Swiss Valais, the Italian Valle d'Aosta, where Souches Mères is grown, gets hot in the summer. Yet there's an echo of the nearby glaciers, for all that, and certainly there's the thermal cool of mountain nights, and so the wine gives an impression of tenderness even with its 14 percent alcohol.

When you taste a wine like this, you learn something certain: such a thing doesn't just happen. Who knows what accord exists between these 106-year-old vines and the ground in which they live? It is easy to imagine Giulio walking deliberately through the vineyard, observing, listening. You can taste it, not by knowing where to look but by understanding the overtones that peal around a wine so hale, so gentle and affectionate. You bring a calmness to them that you may not have known was in you. You sit in the kindness of your friend's table, and yet the wine takes you elsewhere, and for a moment you're alone, solitary and pure. Altered, you return to the feast, thinking, *What a world this is.* And isn't that what we should be talking about when we talk about wine?

The last two wines I drank while writing this chapter were a Champagne, a basic nonvintage from a producer called Doyard-Mahé, in Vertus, and a Scheurebe Spätlese from 2001, made by Hans-Günter Schwarz at the estate Müller-Catoir. Here is how I responded to each of them.

The Champagne was an ordinary competent citizen of very good land. It was all Vertus, a Premier Cru in the Côte des Blancs. It seemed to have been based on a lean vintage, which accounted for its sinewy, almost diffident attack. The first night it tasted a little shrill; the following night it had fleshed out somewhat, but even then, though it was good, it wasn't *fine.* My image-tone for it was, "This is a nice shirt and looks good on me but it's also scratchy and I won't be sad to take it off." If someone asked me what it tasted like, I'd say it was appley, didn't seem very ripe, indeed a little lean and bracing, but with an echo of cool fruit, an okay Champagne for hot weather or perhaps with briny, coppery oysters. It had no great resonance, but it was pleasant to sip it outside that second evening, in the company of the local birds.

It was worth drinking. Its good facets were worth pausing before and appreciating. But it wasn't worth cherishing.

The other wine was the 2001 Scheurebe Spätlese, and to this

I brought a great deal of memory and emotion before the first glass was poured.

It was the final vintage for the great cellar master of modern times, not just in Germany but everywhere—Hans-Günter Schwarz. His thirty-ninth harvest. He retired a few years prematurely, as it happened, and in difficult circumstances, and this vintage was his swan song. He had become a friend, and it was elegiac when we first tasted it on an afternoon in early 2002, sampling these last wines he made.

His great vintage was 1998, as perfect and beautiful as a crop could be. The 2001 was licking at its heels but fell the tiniest bit short. We knew we'd never stop debating which were the very greatest wines Hans-Günter made, '01 or '98?

When we tasted the Scheurebe, though, there was no discussion. This was the ne plus ultra. I will never forget the feeling of absurd, miraculous good fortune we all felt when we tasted that wine. It doesn't matter what you do, how you prepare, what virtues you have cultivated—the gods give such gifts when they deign to, for reasons they keep to themselves.

I wrote the word "Matterhorn" in my tasting book that first time. When I was a young pup, my then wife and I went to Zermatt for a few days one September, and it rained and rained. People said there were mountains and we believed them, but we couldn't see them. On the third day we were distressed to see that the latest forecast was calling for yet more rain, and wearily we yielded to the disappointment of writing off the trip.

That night I was up to pee, and an odd light was coming in through the curtains. On the way back to bed I pulled the curtain aside and saw the Matterhorn lit by a huge full moon. It wasn't supposed to have happened. The gods had relented. The day broke suddenly clear. We greedily devoured the mountains and the sunlight. But that first view of the strange mystic Matterhorn veiled in new snow, a ghost bride looming into the black sky—that was a visitation from a strange unnerving grace.

Which is why I wrote the word "Matterhorn" in my book

that day, tasting that wine. The feeling returned, and I knew its name.

I don't think I'd tasted the wine since then. But an almost ten-year-old Scheurebe—it was just the right time.

I didn't really remember the wine viscerally; I rather had the cinematic memory-of-the-memory of having loved it. So when I poured it, all that went through my mind was, *This oughta be good.* But oh, that first sniff . . .

All I could think of was a vision of seeing a woman you once loved but with whom things didn't work out, for any of a thousand reasons, and you haven't seen her for years and years and it's not like she haunts your very soul anymore. It's been forever. And the instant you lay eyes on her it whams into you again, like a tide that moves your cells in her direction, and it isn't logical and it can't possibly be helped, but suddenly you're incandescent. That's how it was to take that first sniff of wine.

In just an instant the world falls away. The dross of the world dissolves, and in its wake is a charged, silent clarity. I thought right away of Hans-Günter. He was the high priest of Scheurebe, possessing all its wizardly mysteries, able to conjure the gods with it. These wines were unsentimental and powerful, replete with esoteric secrets, deadly sharp and cunning. No one has made them remotely as well, and so this wine in my glass was a sort of leave-taking. A glass of beauty and *tristesse.*

Initially there is a shock that such beauty exists at all. We always feel it, just as we always forget its power until the next time it happens. It's over in an instant, yet it is unbelievable. The wine was still absurdly vital, beyond expressive, as if I were looking at Niagara Falls without any sound, just the amazing mass of plunging water and the shimmer around it, in eerie silence.

First the flavor reached upward. The acidity was ravishing, and the little tingle of CO_2 was a splash of ridiculous freshness. All the angular loveliness of Scheurebe was there: cassis, sage, roasted pineapple, pink grapefruit, passionfruit, and malt, all curling upward like the writhing flame of a blown-out candle. Yet all of it was graceful, the stretching of dancer limbs, the morning-glory tendrils reaching around the branch, and it was this I remembered from the first time, as well as the wickedly exquisite poise of fruit sweetness with the grape's innate sourness, like the flaw that makes a face not just pretty but beautiful. I sat with the wine in a state of amazement. And then a curious thing happened.

As it warmed in my glass, as it took a little oxygen, the arching high notes began to soften and dissolve, and a miracle of melting began, as though the wine were in some slow swoon, and I felt I saw a core there, something I had hardly ever seen. I started repeating the (pretty dumb) mantra *It's all about the melting,* because I wanted to lock it in somewhere, I didn't want it to go away until I understood it appreciatively. Melting, I thought . . . like drowsing down to sleep, like surrendering; after the fruit is finished putting on its gorgeous show, it sits with you and puts its head on your shoulder, and in some fine strange way you are given to each other. In that moment there is no line between "me" and "the wine." All of it is bliss and the sadness that follows bliss.

That was not only a wine worth drinking, it was a moment of meaning in a life worth living.

Between these poles—a good-enough, quite okay wine and a transcendently beautiful wine—lives a big world of all kinds of worthwhile wines. There's never the time to drink them all. So I ask myself, how do I want wines to be?

One can make a list of certain attributes; in fact I've done just that in another part of this book. But I think it can be reduced to two essential qualities: I want wines to be refreshing and companionable. I do not need my blocks busted and I don't find being blown away always to be entirely pleasant. I like wines that embody quietude, because quiet contains more than noise, which contains only itself.

Moving deeper into the more ethereal attributes that I hope

for in a wine, I would identify, first, beauty of various magnitudes. Big beauty is regal, resplendent, magnificent. Little beauty is exquisite, refined, delicate. There's a place for them all, though I'm especially partial to the wee ones. And once in a great while you get a wine like that Catoir Scheurebe in which the difference between big and little beauty isn't so much split as dissolved. That wine had both deep capacity and intimate tenderness.

Wine can also be a source of mystery and evanescence. It doesn't happen often, and it seems never to happen if you demand or summon it. All you can hope is to be ready. So that when a wine suddenly speaks to an inner child you thought you had lost, or to a friendly angel you've been neglecting, you are able to pause and slip through the portal as it beckons you.

For instance, Eiswein, an ultra-concentrated sweet wine made from harvesting deeply frozen grapes, can approach the limits of ethereality. At one point I responded with markedly strong emotion to a young Eiswein at Johannes Leitz's estate in Rüdesheim, and I did a little astral travel, both feeling the emotion and observing myself feeling it.

It's easy and plausible to suppose I'm responding to the exceptional purity of excellent Eiswein. But as soon as I use words I'm in trouble, because I grope for language equal to the power of what I'm feeling, yet the moment I do I start sucking power out of that language, because too many high-chi words are crashing into one another. And the sense of divinity that wines like this convey is best expressed in silence. As soon as I say "divine" and "sublime," I have named the thing but not conveyed the numinous emotion.

So I asked, what is the source of the poignancy I feel? Maybe it *is* poignant to express this ecstatic truth of the world by dint of something frozen. As if in order to learn its truth you have to stop its heart.

All of these things make a wine worth drinking. But the final answer to that question is that we ourselves do. We are the means by which a wine's beauty and meaning become conscious. Sleeping in its silent bottle, a wine is merely potential energy, inchoate. When we meet a wine's authenticity with our own, we are part of the blossoming.

Yet if we approach a wine demanding to be entertained, blown away, speciously seduced, we meet the wine with that which is most false and infantile within us. The wine doesn't stand a chance. A wine is worth drinking to the extent it is authentic, interesting, and beautiful. We are joined in a crux of joy when we ourselves are grateful, attentive, and engaged.

4

ACCOUNTING FOR TASTE

As a wine writer I can indulge myself among the larger questions, but as a wine merchant—my day job—I buy the stuff and sell it. I do this in a particular way, seeking out wines from a network of small producers in Champagne, Austria, and Germany and selling them to unwary consumers over here. Though I also sell—or propose—an entire way of thinking about wine (which of course encourages people to cozy up to the kinds of wines I like), I sell bottles of wine that others will sell in turn and that everyday folks will someday drink as well. Being a wine merchant first and foremost is a useful grounding, especially for a guy like me who's prone to abstraction.

The abstractions I refer to—some of which you've read about in the previous chapter—have never been a priori for me. Rather, they have arisen organically from the choices I have made. I look back and observe, "So *that's* what I was doing," and then I try to put it into words, and then it looks abstract. For instance, if I follow my taste for wines of delicacy, eventually I find myself extolling the basic virtues of delicacy. I seem to be driven to do this. Delicacy is a virtue we often overlook, and I'd like it to take the occasional bow. (Along similar lines I once realized, as I was tasting in Champagne, that all the wines I worked with originated from a narrow band of latitude, roughly from 48° to 50° north. I never sat behind my desk thinking, *I will be the shaman of the vigorous north!* It just happened, because I like the way those wines can balance vigor and delicacy, lightness and intensity. Nor am I opposed to a little self-indulgence.)

Eventually all of your past experiences carve a channel of sorts for you to follow. From time to time I used to offer wines from grower cooperatives, small ones, with good sites and tasty wines at low prices. I couldn't sell them. I had in effect trained my customers to insist on family-made wines, and the co-op items simply didn't engage the buyers' interest, no matter how good they might be. But there was never a point where I told myself, *I must offer only small-batch family-estate wines*, because I never considered otherwise. Those values were my glide path into wine in the first place. There's a saying in Zen: "Whoever discovered water, it wasn't a fish." Every single aspect of my early immersions in wine was—and what a shame this has become a buzzword—artisanal. Now it is thirty-five years later, and with that perspective I can see the big picture, the core values that have informed all my choices, even when I was unaware.

When I started importing wine back in the mid-eighties, there were already several importers whose names were brands, as mine has since become: Robert Chadderdon, Kermit Lynch, Robert Kacher, and Neil Empson, among others, standing atop the shoulders of the true vanguard, people like Frank Schoonmaker and Alexis Lichine, who'd established their businesses not long after the repeal of Prohibition. There was also a fledgling wine press that had discovered a useful angle when writing about wine: profile the importer and advise readers to look for his or her name. Ultimately a wine drinker learned which importer's taste most consistently matched his own, and he'd gravitate toward those merchants. That's why we put our names on the labels. This in turn led to the somewhat precious notion of the celebrity importer, which observers outside the United States have some doubts about.

In my case, I was dealing in a niche category—German

wines—and importing from small growers whom no one had heard of, and so it was a helpful shortcut to brand myself as a means of drawing attention to the growers and their wines. I was part of a wave of new-generation importers, and all of us were helped enormously by the wine press, which created a climate in which we could flourish.

We importers tend to be passionate nerds. We have quirky palates and distinctive points of view, which becomes a useful way of predicting the style of the wine you're thinking of buying. When I'm in Europe and I order wine in a restaurant from a grower I'm not familiar with, I reflexively look for the nonexistent American importer's label, and when I don't find it I'm missing a crucial clue. Because Sally's wines are one way and Peter's wines are another way, and Jasper's wines are some weird hybrid of the first two ways, and Lucy's wines are in a whole new universe, and if I see one of their names on a bottle I start to know what I'll be drinking. We all compile our portfolios based on the kinds of wines we ourselves love, and so we establish an identity; this guy likes "high acidity" and this woman likes "lots of oak" and this fellow likes "earthy wine" and so on.

If an importer's a moving target, I doubt he'll do well in the long run.

In addition to serving as guides, we act as gatekeepers. It is understood (or should be) that we have our own standards, and that prior to being sellers we are buyers. We ourselves need to be convinced. Another vital reason for placing my name on the label is to control any impulse I might have to compromise on a selection. I love the growers with whom I work, but once in a while I need to risk incurring their ire by rejecting a wine they want me to offer, or to push for higher quality in what I do offer. I was led by the example of a mentor.

Very early in my career I traveled to France with the star importer Robert Kacher, and I was struck by something I witnessed in Alsace. Kacher had a grower with whom he worked, but he bought none of that grower's basic wines. Instead he bought the reserve wines—the next level up—and offered *them* as the basic wines. He was offering his customers exceptional quality, and if he was concerned about the grower's ego, he subsumed that worry into the larger principle of providing quality and value to his clientele.

This sort of approach can cause some backlash in the country of origin, and I can only do my best to convince a grower that it's in our mutual interest to establish a sustainable reputation for excellence. I have lost growers who thought I was being a big shot. But the best of them see me as a colleague working respectfully toward a common goal.

Customers have sometimes wondered about the wines I rejected. An organization called the German Wine Society once staged a tasting of wines I *didn't* select from growers I imported. Well, hmmm! But to my great relief, the results convinced the tasters that I had indeed screened out the ordinary or the merely good and that the wines I *did* select were exceptional.

Importers don't have to be quite so nitpicky everywhere in the wine world, but this sort of selectivity is crucial in a production culture like Germany's. In other places, a grower may have just a handful of wines—say, two whites, a rosé, and three reds. This makes it relatively easy for an importer to decide whether to work with him; either he's consistently good or he isn't, and if he isn't, then he doesn't keep his importer. But in Germany it's not so simple. Some growers there may offer three dozen different wines. I can't offer thirty-six wines from any one grower —German wine is unruly enough as it is—so I do my job and screen.

First I screen for raw quality. Then I screen to produce a harmonious offering of sensible size, breadth, and proportion. In the process I run the ever-present risk of annoying the grower, who may not see why anyone should stand between his or her wines and potential customers. Growers have terminated our relationship because of this very thing.

Every grower deserves to be represented with full-hearted conviction, and my loyalty to all of my growers is profound. But it is not paramount. My primary loyalty is, and must be, to my customer. She deserves the utter best I can find for her. If she likes the other guy's palate more than mine, then she buys from him and not from me. But I will delineate my principles, what I cherish and why, and hope to show her that I don't cut corners on quality.

I hear you ask, *Really? Never?* And the answer is, I never compromise on raw quality, although I sometimes bend a bit when it comes to my *subjective* judgments about the wine. Some wines don't convince me because of my own proclivities, but if they're fascinating, then I won't block them. I will, though, express my hesitation about the wine and let the customer decide. (This sort of transparency, which feels to me like ordinary candor, is crucial for any wine lover, and it's a subject I return to in the next chapter.)

I'm also mindful that too much focus on principles can sound either precious or unseemly. But I seem to be the only importer who describes in detail what I look for and what I seek to avoid. I don't want customers to have to *infer,* "Oh, that's a Terry wine." I want to be emphatic: if you buy from me, you will obtain this kind of wine and not that one.

There's a broader lesson here: you can't consider the question of tasting, or of taste, without learning to map your subjectivities. Years ago in my sales literature I wrote a thorough section along the lines of "the kinds of wines I like, and why," because I knew I wouldn't be useful to my reader (and customer) if I didn't clearly announce my preferences. (It continues to astonish me that most importers—and critics!—do not do the same. Are we to infer the kinds of wines you like by tasting your whole portfolio for years and years?) Similarly, good wine merchants, whether retailers or sommeliers, have learned to ask this most salient question: What was the last wine you really liked? If you can answer it and, even better, say *why*, they'll know exactly what to offer you. (Reviewers should do this also; I make that case in more detail down the road.)

Here's how that would look, using my subjectivities as an example. Useful, right?

Companionable: I like a wine that's hale and good company. It doesn't indulge in monologue. It doesn't vent. It's chipper and engaging.

Accommodating: I like a wine that lets the rest of your life get a word in edgewise now and again.

Refreshing: I like to keep sipping it, and I can't if it starts to dull my palate rather than to refresh it.

Interesting: I like there to be something in the flavor that's worth noticing and considering, whether a lot or a little.

Attractive: Not necessarily pretty, but obviously *pleasant* in some basic way.

Distinctively Itself: I am bored with anonymous-tasting wine. Tell me who you are.

Our wine culture seems to be exceptionally, robustly healthy, thanks at least in part to this ad hoc scrum of importers offering wines that ignite our passions and create a lively dialogue about the larger issues in play. But only if we talk about them!

My wines were outliers. The categories with which I worked were unpopular. Outlier wines and the people who advocate them can be catnip for wine writers. I was also quick with a quip. If being a "wine personality" was helpful to my growers, then that's what I'd be. It wasn't entirely disagreeable, and I'm grateful for it, but it wasn't the thing that moved me. If we had a bad year I'd slink like a guilty dog into my growers' cellars the following year, and if we did well I'd arrive on a glowing white steed. What always motivated me was being their champion. I admired and loved them, and I wanted the whole world to agree. If I had to become part of the story, then so be it.

In retrospect, it isn't remarkable that I gravitated toward the wines I liked and away from the ones I didn't. We all do it. You'll probably think it's crazy if I add that wines gravitate toward the people who'll appreciate them. Of course I don't mean that literally. But wines and the people who drink them eventually form mutually comfortable relationships. For myself, it's not only comfortable but *comforting*. I am reassured by the very existence of the wines I love. At first we seek out more of the wines that made us happy — that's logical enough — yet eventually I think those wines can actually form our tastes. Nor do they stop there; they can also help form our temperaments and aesthetic frames of reference, because repeated exposure seems to deepen our intuitive accord with a certain way of rendering beauty.

It is also self-evident that no two tasters are identical. But what does that matter? I tend to drink wine with people who share my taste, at least generally, and yet even if two of us are sharing a wine we both feel is great, we may well have different reasons for our impressions. I could say, "It is great because it is mysterious," and she could say, "It is great because it is adamant and explicit," and it's futile to try to reconcile those views. It's far more useful and fascinating to consider both our broad neighborhood of agreement and then the little houses of sensibility that each of us inhabits alone.

It is always helpful to know one's own taste. It's even more helpful to be able to describe it. And it's most helpful of all to stay alert to the ineluctable changes in our tastes as we go through life. The more we drink wine, the larger and richer our frames of reference become, because we have an ever-deepening context for each new wine we receive. Our bodies change, too. As we get older we're more likely to be inadequately hydrated, which affects the physical properties of our mouths. If our sense of smell is diminished, we compensate by practicing greater powers of concentration. For myself, tasting has become much quicker, whereas drinking has become much slower. That is, if I am appraising I can do it in a flash, but if I am drinking I like to slow down enough to see the wine's deliberate evolution as the bottle slowly empties.

Don't let your taste ossify. It will play tricks on you, and you risk a cognitive dissonance between what you've determined you like versus what you find yourself liking despite yourself.

I believe there are two elements in play when you wish to understand your taste, or someone else's. These overlap like a Venn diagram, although there are zones where they don't intersect, and it's apropos to consider them separately.

The first element is the actual physical tongue. This bit of physiology is by no means static. It changes quickly according to a host of short-term circumstances, and it changes slowly as part of the overall changes in a person's body over time. For example, when I am jet-lagged I am also dehydrated, and at those times my palate craves *gras*—richness, juiciness—and it is oversensitive to salt and to acidity. If I need to taste under those conditions—the first days of a buying trip in Europe come to mind—I have learned to allow for those changes and adjust my appraisals.

Once you're aware of those kinds of sensitivities it's hard to tune them out, and you go a little mad. My palate is one way if the weather's dry and another way if it's humid, one way if I'm rested and another way if I'm tired, one way in clear (that is, high-pressure) weather and another in rainy weather, one way in the morning and another way in the afternoon. This all pertains to my professional palate, I hasten to add. As a drinker I'm easy-peasy. (Nor do I drink much wine in the morning.) But as a *taster* I need to be aware of my persnickety palate. It can preoccupy a dude if you let it.

I am notorious for not eating lunch on tasting days, much to the chagrin of anyone traveling with me, who eventually learns to pack sandwiches from the breakfast spread. I'm also ridiculously careful at breakfast; one itty-bitty slice of smoked salmon will falsify my palate for several hours. I'm militantly against chives for similar reasons. Growers work a whole year to show me wines I'll taste for one or two minutes. The least I can do is take care that my palate isn't screwed up.

I suspect that beginning tasters are not aware of such things, nor do they need to be. But anyone who is (and remains) seriously interested in wine shouldn't breezily assume that his palate is static and immutable, any more than a young pitcher should presume that he'll always be able to throw 95 mph.

But taste is only partly determined by a tongue; we also taste with every quirk and warp of our proclivities and dispositions. We inhabit each other, our palates and us. The actual physical sensorium by which we apprehend flavor is merely the outer skin of how we taste, because we are *who we are* as we taste. And who we are changes like a madman regardless of whether we want it to. Indeed, in a subsequent chapter I argue that we taste with the sum total of everything that has happened to us that day, because our "palate" isn't some little bot who steps discretely out of our bodies. It is the sum of all the things we are, tasting something.

All importers are obviously different, and I'd never presume to speak for all of us. For me, when I taste a wine from one of my suppliers, these are the elements in play, the "proper" (or basic) ones first:

Is it good? That's actually not enough. Is it outstanding of its type?

Can I honestly assert that it is worth the asking price?

Is it necessary? Sometimes a good wine is too similar to other wines I offer, and I'd rather avoid redundancy.

And then come the ancillary concerns I wish I could banish but probably can't. Is this the new vintage of a wine that sold well last year? (That puts me under pressure to offer it, because it will be an easy sale. The grower is also anticipating selling me what he sold me the previous year.) Is this a wine that the producer wants or needs to sell? (This puts me into a diplomatic bind, because I really want to make them happy.) Pragmatically speaking, one shouldn't be too picky with one's suppliers. They have their own needs, and they want my loyalty. Yet one also has one's customers to consider. My conscience can be clear only if I am telling the truth, not because I'm so morally precious but because it sucks to sell things you don't believe in. I'm fallible and I make mistakes, but I do mean what I say; I think the wine is good. "Yes, but you're not objective" is a misconstruction of what objectivity is and whether it is germane to the moment. I'm not supposed to be objective, I'm supposed to be rigorous and professional.

Wine is an aesthetic object, and these are inimical to objectivity. This doesn't mean we can't be objective at all, just that we need to recognize the ineluctable line between that and our inevitable subjectivities.

Let me put it this way. Supposing I had a really spicy expressive dry Muscat on the table and a few tasters were evaluating it. *Objectively* we could agree—the wine is dry, the wine is fresh, the wine is blatantly aromatic. But someone doesn't like the smell of Muscat at all, and the best this taster could say is, "It's an acceptable example of a genre I happen to despise." Another taster is a cerebral sort of person and finds most Muscats too simple. Yet another taster—that would be me—rejoices precisely in that simplicity, and so one person says, "This wine is delightful" while another says, "This wine is crude and overemphatic," and the reader throws up her hands, thinking, *These so-called experts can't agree! Why can't they just be objective?* And yet they can be—up to the point I described.

Is that point at all useful to the rest of us? Yes and no. For example, if a taster happens to be highly sensitive to acidity, he will experience as "shrill" some wines that other tasters will find to be "vivid." Or one taster loves the (sometimes) earthy aromas and flavors of natural-yeast fermented wines while another is put off by what she experiences as an unpleasant funkiness.

If this is confusing to readers of tasting notes and wine evaluations, they need to be asking more salient questions. It isn't *Consumer Reports* comparing dishwashers or vacuum cleaners. That's where we need objectivity. In wine reviewing, what we need to demand is for writers to come clean about their subjectivities. If we critics and commentators are to be useful to you, we can't affect some spurious objectivity. What we can do is know our palates, explain our palates to you, clarify what we're warm and cold to, and not make you have to guess.

This, to me, is the first obligation of a critic, and not only a wine critic. We need to release ourselves from all the worthless cant about our Imperial Impartiality and instead offer you a consistent, visible, and explicable *subjectivity*. If my readers can say, "Sure, Theise is foaming and frothing over this wine, but come on, that's his type of wine," then I've done my job and we're all better off.

If you have someone to coach you along, a kind of mentor of wine, you'll quickly establish the things you prefer. If you're flying solo, as I did, you'll have to give it time and pay attention. There isn't a shortcut. If you're a casual drinker and don't care very much, then you'll have to enjoy stumbling around in the mist. You're like Harold and his purple crayon: you're drawing your road as you walk on it. If you think this is fun, welcome to wine.

Here's something useful you can do. Next time you stumble upon a wine you *really* like, take it back to the store and show it to the salesperson (assuming you bought it from a good wine shop, of course), saying, "I'm in love with this wine. Sell me something really similar and sell me something really different." Then open the wines and think about them and about your impressions. Repeat about twenty thousand times! Wine's a moving target, you know; it won't keep still. But it's not just dodging and weaving—it's dancing.

Blind tasting is often touted as a panacea for the ostensible "problem" of subjectivity. Tasting blind, people will tell you, is a guarantor of objectivity. I'm sorry, it isn't. It's just a winged unicorn of fantasy. It merely guarantees that a taster won't be swayed by knowing the reputation of a place or a grower. Let's assume this is true, for argument's sake. No one ever talks about the collateral damage this approach entails. Bluntly, blind tasting results in a ton of mistakes, often laughable mistakes. Let's say you have lined up a bunch of Austrian Rieslings and you're tasting them blind. Let's say you're forbidden to alter your notes (or your scores) when the wines are identified. Let's say there are growers whose wines are often muted after bottling—right when you're tasting them—while other, lesser wines may be quite expressive because they aren't as concentrated. You are at great risk of overrating the simpler wines and underrating the higher-class wines. It ain't theoretical, folks; it happens many, *many* times every year. And yet these luckless wines are assigned an absolute value—the "points" they are "awarded."

True Believers in this fatuous approach will protest that this risk is far less than the risk that wines may be overrated because tasters approach them with awe or expectations of greatness. Really? Then I'd say those tasters have no business anywhere in print, because they are insufficiently professional. And the product they provide us is shallow and denuded, because it can depict only how wines "perform" in the context of blind tastings, which they tell us we must believe are the only road to pure truth. Well, bollocks to that. Blind tastings are certainly a particular environment in which wines may be judged or ranked, but they create their own distortions, and they enfeeble the hapless humanoids tasked with deciding the absolute quality of wines whose identities are kept secret.

Far too much energy is squandered pursuing this chimera of

objectivity. A writer whom I respect greatly has said it's impossible to be objective about a wine estate if you've accepted a junket to see them at their expense. I don't think that is quite true. It's *difficult,* to be sure, but that's because you hesitate to criticize your hosts for fear of being churlish or ungracious, despite the fact that this was a risk they freely chose to take when they invited you. It was a business decision, not a social one.

The writer is free to decide she doesn't like the wines. She is even free to determine that the winery isn't important enough to write about at all. It's actually more awkward if she *does* like the wines, because if she says so in print, she is open to accusations that she couldn't possibly have been objective since the winery paid her way. She becomes the victim of our romantic notions of objectivity.

Am I myself less objective about my selections because a grower opens old wines for me or picks up the check at dinner? Here's a little story; please judge for yourself.

One afternoon in March a few years ago, I stood with several colleagues in the small private cellar of Laurent Champs, of Champagne Vilmart & Cie. Laurent allowed us to choose the wines we wished to taste, or really to drink. Our "work" was finished. Now it was time to smack our collective lips with a few old wines.

I lobbied to taste the least remarkable wines in the cellar, but there's nothing at Vilmart that isn't remarkable, as I ought to have known. It's just that the heavy-hitter wines Laurent often makes are the kinds that show up in everyone's tastings. They're featured alongside other wines assuming the attribute of greatness. This comes dangerously close to making a commodity of greatness, and I like to talk to the orphans. They get less attention.

In any case, the four of us stood shoulder to shoulder by a small table, and as the wines proceeded I felt a kind of intimacy settle over the room, the sort that children feel when they and their friends are hiding from someone. Perhaps we were also hiding—from the quotidian world outside, drinking a friend's old wines, enveloped in gratitude and happiness.

I was originally led to Vilmart by the effusions of a wine writer, but once I walked in the door I wasn't disposed one way or another, except to hope that the wines were good. In fact they were, but in those early days I had some concerns that a few of the wines were too oaky. Luckily for me, Laurent Champs was (and is) a civilized, smart, and gracious man, and we could speak collegially. I have known him twenty years now, and watched his wines proceed through an apotheosis into a new divinity they often convey.

Each year as I arrive at Vilmart I find I have a feeling of anticipation and pleasure similar to the way I feel walking into the great German estate of Dönnhoff. Yet once I'm actually tasting, none of this is present anymore. Then it is only the wines. And when they again are beautiful, I feel like I'm breathing my own air, because they have reached the level of making it look easy, that lit-from-within quality, serene and lapidary. Very few wines have it. It makes me feel at home.

It's not that the wines are always calm and serene. Sometimes they're frisky and even hyper, in vintages prone to be jittery. Yet even then they offer the flavor of homecoming, belonging, gliding into a calm harbor of welcome. They can be animated, but they're never flirtatious. They seem to have already accepted you; they are loving. This is part of a larger existential meaning to Vilmart, having to do with the circumstances of Laurent's father's life and the way these things ramify for Laurent and for his wines. The gleam they have around them isn't an accident.

I keep returning to "beautiful." We don't often hear this word in wine-speak, and I can't really say why. It might be similar to the absence of the word "delicious" in most published tasting notes. We seem to approach wine as if it were a sudoku puzzle we had to solve analytically. On the other hand, when we respond spontaneously and sensually to wine, our feelings can't help but engage. There are plenty of impressive wines and even exciting wines that aren't necessarily beautiful. Some wines that certain tasters describe as "hedonistic" are merely gaudy and lurid. Beauty, though, seems like a prerequisite for profundity, and I mean true profundity, not just the effect of significance by virtue of mere brute power. (If you only yell loud enough, people will think you have something important to say.) I promise you, if you started thinking of wine in terms of beauty, even for just a day, you'd find yourself starting over. Most of what you know —or "know"—won't at all be useful.

Whatever knowledge you've accumulated about this region, this grape, this grower—in short, your entire training—will not pertain now. You'll struggle to understand what is happening. But if you can stop and just relax, you may feel the presence of a certain silence. The ever-present thrum is absent, the grinding background buzz of just coping. The wine in your glass is a psalm. Everything everyone says is wonderful. You're dissolving and you feel a little foolish, and yet you hardly feel you have to say a word.

When you know these things—that feelings and history and culture and meanings orbit so very many wines—you will bring more of yourself to the lip of the glass. Not only is this a decent habit of living, it also gives you a stay against burnout. It becomes a well you can drink from when you're feeling parched, and the water will always be clean and cold.

In short, you cultivate the richest possible *subjectivity*. You are more entirely yourself. For instance, I know I am someone who responds to wines like Vilmart's as they become not more intense but gentler. Not more voluminous but more breathy. Not more brilliant but more gleaming; not more energetic but more consoling. How do you even hear these frequencies if you're twisting your hapless self into some conniption of "objectivity"?

We do not, any of us, have time to squander on such non-sense. A universe of reverie is at hand, waiting for us to just re-lax, figure out what sort of selves we are, and then be them.

We need to know who we bring to the glass before we can truly receive what the glass brings to us. This may seem to con-tradict a point I make elsewhere, that the best way to taste is to forget ourselves. But the only way to reach the point of self-for-getting is to know ourselves so entirely that it becomes inter-nalized. Anyone who plays an instrument knows exactly what I mean. Virtuosos don't need to consider technique consciously or discretely. It is there for them. Similarly, a virtuosic taster isn't merely (or at all) a person who can blind-guess a wine in fifteen seconds; he is someone who no longer fusses about palate at all, someone who receives a wine directly, unfiltered, immediately, and too fast for words.

And we are changelings, all through our lives and in any given moment. If I register the changes in my palate, I must also account for changes in my basic state of being. For instance, it seems to have been established that men in middle age begin to produce more of a hormone that is linked to melancholy. I'm not a lugubrious type myself, but I was relieved to have a tangi-ble reason to resist the tyranny of cheerfulness I felt the world imposed upon me and to assert the perquisites of my temper-ament. In private moments I am prone to reverie. I'm always pleased when someone admits to not being relentlessly positive. I think that happiness has only partly to do with joy. I like to see faces in repose. All of this plays into my appreciation of the pen-umbral, the tenebrous, the easing into darkness and peace. It's why I love old wines, gentle wines, tender wines, and it's why I receive them more fully than I did before.

We learn ourselves better as we get older. There are fewer unmapped places within us. Our skin starts to fit correctly. And if this self-comfort is easy, it can be absorbed, and we needn't think about who is receiving a wine; we already know quite well. This enables me to relax and receive, and to escape the prison of self-consciousness. The wine slips easily in. I slide toward it with no effort. I am merely and simply open. Ruefully I recall my beginner's days, when I was like a cobra poised to strike every wine that came to me. It was crucial to find a place for each wine in the schemata I was urgently constructing. My mind was frantic to categorize, to establish contexts, to place wines on a mental map: What linked to what, which wines were cousins, siblings, even twins? What was salient and what was ancillary? What were the natures of these wines—were they cerebral like Bordeaux (in those days at least) or corporeal like Burgundy? Were they suave like Champagne, countrified and tart like Tuscan reds (in those days!), and were they fantastically vivid and yet thrillingly incomprehensible like Riesling? Oh, my poor palate was a busy, busy beast. In time I learned how to get out of my own way. When crucial wines come to me now, I've left the porch light on for them.

I'm not actually sure I have a "good palate," but I'm very sure I bring an interesting person to the glass. Often I wonder if my literal palate is among the less acute on the spectrum, because others appear to be receiving more than I do, and I've made my share of mistakes over the years. My own palate, such as it is, does well interpreting the ways a wine behaves, the kind of temperament it seems to have, the shape and torque of its motion and the ways its various acts are organized—"acts" in the sense of dramatic arcs such as exposition, development, denouement. That's the stuff I get. I'm not especially sensitive to volatile acidity; I pick up Brettanomyces (which cause the barnyard aroma) but don't mind them if the wine isn't repugnantly fecal. I'm sensitive to TCA (which makes wines taste corked, like wet cardboard), but it's my wife who's our resident cork bloodhound.

I have an entirely okay palate, but nothing more. But I manage as a taster because my effort of concentration is formidable, my mind and heart are free-ranging, I have good judgment, and —most important—I know how to relax.

I worry that the capacity to relax with wine is being ritually pounded out of people in the "somm" nexus. I mean, you know, flashcards. But I also need to admit that I actually don't know a lot about wine, or, more accurately, about wines. At some point I realized I was lagging behind my fellow wine peeps in the quantity of information I'd accumulated and could remember. But I also realized what I'd have to do to collect and retain that information: squander a life. It's one thing if wine's your *idée fixe,* but while I was deeply drawn to wine and absorbed in it, life was larger than any one preoccupation. So I quit trying to be a generalist and chose to become a specialist, to go deep where my passions were most abidingly stirred.

I have a high regard for wine people who have internalized far more information than I ever did or ever could—or ever wished to. I also sometimes wonder what it all amounts to. I once heard there was a question on the Master Sommelier test about the purpose of the flimsy little wire net you used to see on old bottles of Rioja. Can this be true? I mean, how many times will you ever need this ephemera at the table? It may be interesting, I suppose, to have memorized all thirteen grape varieties permitted in Châteauneuf-du-Pape—though no guest will ever ask—but my own approach would be to visit the place and soak it in, its climate, soil, what kind of people make wine there, who came before them. From that I might hope to understand why there were thirteen permitted grapes in the first place, and why some of them were white, and this seems to matter more than to have memorized their names.

There is a line—and not a fine line, a big thick line—between accumulating information and deriving understanding. The average wine person has much more information stored than I do, but I have at least as much *knowledge* as he does, and maybe more. If I'm right—if—then a curious theory begins to form. Normally things look bigger when we study them close up. But the obsessive study of wine seems to make it *smaller,* because we've put it into a small suffocating room and shut out the rest of life. Wine is a being of beauty, and it needs space, and room to breathe. If we interrogate it, it may indeed confess, but its confession won't be the whole truth.

Perhaps there's a link between an obsessive approach to wine and the kinds of wines that seem obsessive themselves. I have had wines that seemed to clamor, that seemed to need to assure me, "I am obsessed with showing you how *quirky* I am!" And by the way, it's not like I'm any sort of master of divine aesthetics; I played guitar for decades, and I have liked what are now called "shredders," guys who play a lot of notes. I still like virtuosity, but not for its own sake; now I care about which of those notes are music and which are the noise of the player's ego. Nor does sheer volume mean anything to me. *I can't play well but I can play LOUD* is a cordial invitation for me to leave the damn room. I get to be ashamed because I used to be that guy . . . but an aesthetic preference for delicacy and restraint can apply to many things—among them, as we're about to see, wine.

5
POWER AT ALL COSTS?

I want sommeliers to like me, and mostly they do. Mostly. Recently I dined at a sweet little place in the Italian Alps that I knew had a good wine program, watched over by the coproprietor, who ran the sixteen-seat restaurant with her life partner, the chef. I looked over her list and it was smart. I could easily have chosen cool wines from it, but I wanted to pay her the compliment of asking her to select for my wife and me.

At such times it helps to articulate your tastes and describe the kinds of wines you like. I said, "Surprise us, but please let me explain that I like precise wines more than powerful wines, lacy wines more than creamy wines . . ." And as I went on speaking her smile grew wider and she nodded her head in accord. "I don't mind big strong wines," I continued, "but I like focus even more, and I'm willing to sacrifice some power to get it."

"Yes, yes," she concurred. "We like the same kinds of wines. I know exactly what to bring you."

"Well, then—" I began.

"I think people like us should breed!" she declaimed.

"Excuse me?"

"We need to people the world with civilized drinkers who like delicate wines!" Ah, now I saw where she was going with this.

"Yeah, yeah, it could be a kind of Tinder . . ." I was warming to the idea. We were having . . . oh, what do they call it? Chemistry, right? At least it seemed that way until I went and ruined it. As she made to leave the table, I peeped up, "Just one more thing. Can we have alcohol no higher than thirteen and a half percent?"

Clouds of dismay crossed her face. "Ah . . . that will be a constraint, a serious constraint."

"I know," I said, "and I'm sorry. But what can I do? I didn't make this world—I'm just trying to stay sober. Hell, I'm just trying to stay *awake.*"

There went the spring in her step. Thus furrowed her brow. In the end we drank very well, but I wondered whether I'd annoyed her.

I am getting really weary of having to insist, everywhere I go, that I do not want high-alcohol wines. But I have to be strict. If I say my limit is 14 percent, they'll bring me something they swear is 14.2 percent and they're sure I'll love it, and I never ever do. So I have become something of a pill.

(This apart from the fact I'd rather not drink beer, cocktails, mead, cider, sake, or tea with my meal. I love tea—I have a pot going now as I write—but when I sit down to eat I'd like wine please, thank you.)

On the face of it, it's silly to demarcate at 14 percent, but it's arbitrary wherever one draws one's line, and north of 14 percent the odds that I'll enjoy a wine shrink away nearly to nothing. Of course I'm aware that I am missing some excellent wines, and I may even be excluding myself from wines I'll actually like. In fact, I know so; a local Spanish place I completely adore offers excellent Fino and Manzanilla Sherries as aperitifs, and everything in me wants to drink them. But I cannot start a meal with a glass (or two) of something with alcohol around 20 percent. People say, "But you don't feel it," and they're right; you don't feel it in the wine, but in about fifteen minutes you'll feel it in your body, which may be jiggy if you'll be at the table until 2 a.m. and then wobble and weave around the corner to your Barcelona loft. Apropos of Spain, I wish I could drink

Priorat, because I'm sure I'd like how it tastes, except that I can't get past all that booze. I'm also aware of the many wines, mostly from hot climates, in which high alcohol is inherent to their basic characters. Châteauneuf-du-Pape springs to mind.

I'm sad to avoid such wines, but you know what? I'm only a little bit sad. I don't often eat food for wines like that, and I don't have especially boisterous friends. Abstractly I know that Châteauneuf-du-Pape is a "significant" wine and one I "ought" to know. But it's only one little life, and I truly do not need to spend it showing the gods how open-minded I am.

So, okay, why 14 percent? Because much more often than not, something that I don't like happens to (especially but not only) white wines at and above that level. I find it vulgar. I call it the flavor of *coarse* ripeness. If there's a chemical explanation I do not know it, but I do know this: the luscious primary fruit of infant white wines can obscure high alcohol, and it's easy to be fooled. In a couple years when the early fruit fades, the alcohol is like a little blowtorch of bitterness and a jalapeño heat that feels like it was grafted onto the wine.

There is a rudeness to this sort of flavor. It asserts to a point of irritation. It feels loud, distorted, and quite often it leaves a nasty medicinal aftertaste. I accept flavor that speaks, and I relish flavor that sings, but I hate flavor that yells. And I've found that high-alcohol wines give me the opposite qualities from those I seek: equipoise, harmony, civility, and tenderness.

This is not a hard-and-fast rule, mind you, because wine doesn't have those; it only has tendencies and probabilities. Now and again I find myself surprised and even spellbound by a wine above my limit. It would make me sheepish if I didn't already know that it could happen; it is simply unlikely to. And yet from time to time it does.

One night, for example, I was served a wine I didn't want to drink. This was because it had 14 percent alcohol. My host was aware of this inconvenience of mine, but he wanted to serve the wine and promised, "If you don't like it, we'll drink something else." I wanted to be an agreeable guest (and a half-decent friend) and so I accepted the offering.

It was Italian, from the Valle d'Aosta. It was bottle number 401 from a mighty production of 413 bottles. At that point I'd never heard of the estate, ViniRari, or its proprietor, Giulio Moriondo, but I learned that he was a kind of curator of autochthonous (that is, original to the place from which they come, and usually not found beyond that place) grape varieties from the valley, and the wine now in my glass was a field blend from ungrafted vines planted in 1906. It was called Souches Mères, or "mother vines," the genetic material from which other plants are reproduced. The *cuvée* couldn't be determined; my host suggested that "Moriondo himself probably doesn't know what all's in there." No vintage appeared on the label. I was intrigued, albeit warily.

But with the first sniff I felt as transported as I've ever felt with a wine. It smelled at first like decomposing leaves, a sweet late-autumn smell I'd just experienced several days earlier, on a walk through our nearby arboretum. When a fragrance is evocative yet indistinct—when it doesn't specify its cognate (such as lemons or peaches or salami or whatever)—it seems to bypass the normal analytical faculty and go straight to your imagination, and from there you climb aboard the fugue state directly to your soul.

This has happened to me enough that I know what it is each new time, and it was happening now. It really is a kind of carrying-away. The wine seems to envelop you in its odd new silence, and you are suddenly removed from everything immediately around you and taken someplace else. You land in the dark and steer toward whatever you want to be closer to, the haunting aroma or the curiously beautiful music of the flavor. Sniffing the glass again, I sensed the smell of chimney smoke, which alongside the sweet leaf decay composed a sort of portrait of the eerie yet comforting melancholy of this season, the moment before the first snows, the last breaths of ruddiness and gold.

With time in the glass, the Souches Mères started to smell like a warm bath strewn with rose petals, and I had a moment of appreciating the comedy of such disparate things to smell and to sense. Or maybe not so disparate, as these are all smells of dying, the leaves dying on the ground, the petals dying in the bath, the wood dying as it burns. Maybe I laughed to myself because I was uneasy. Death and beauty often walk arm in arm, after all.

The Souches Mères was a revelation, in other words—but for every bottle like it, there are forty-nine bottles that pall and irritate with crude overripe sourness. I was reminded of this recently with a bottle of Lagrein that ought to have been good, except it wasn't.

I like to drink Lagrein when I'm in the Italian Alps. It has that spicy, almost ferrous character I appreciate. (When I'm at home I prefer Austrian Blaufränkisch, which is similar but better.) Lagrein used to be reliably midweight and driven by fruit and mineral flavors. Much of it still is—and yet . . . After several good bottles on different evenings, we ordered another Lagrein at a simple place that brings your bottle to the table already opened. Unpretentious—no worries. But this was a formidable-looking object, heavy, Burgundy-shaped, and when I looked at the back label—*gulp!*—14 percent.

I couldn't really send it back; I had no reason to. The wine was faultless. I just didn't like it. Nor was it the kind of place where one sends wine back unless the wine is seriously corked or has dead bugs in it. So we sipped at it. It was Lagrein with affectations. It had that so-called international flavor—big, sweet, overripe, buxom, callipygian, could have been anything. But I wanted Lagrein!

Poor frustrated me. But this isn't only my problem. This sad specimen represents a trend sweeping the wine world, and it isn't wholesome or salubrious: too often there is too much damn ripeness. I'm not at all sure you can have wines that are both highly ripe and refreshing. Nor will this bother you if you don't want your wines to refresh. But that's how I want them. Even if I'm eating a fat juicy steak I don't crave a fat juicy wine. I want a little relief from all the adipose wobbles of flavor. Some fruit! And I'm sorry, but dates, prunes, raisins—these things are laxatives, not fruit.

How we got here is an interesting question. Where we go from here is even more interesting. Because the issue of ripeness constitutes a prominent segment of a great dialectic in the wine world. It touches upon the suitability of a given grape to a given place and how this is shape-shifting as climate changes; it touches on manipulation of wine, since the final alcohol can be adjusted by various means; and it touches on a basic debate about how we want wine to be. Is it a big gaudy show being put on for us, or is it a fellow being acting as a suitable companion?

The prevailing "popular-kid" style of wine of the past couple decades was big-fruit, high-alcohol hedonistic, and it only stands to reason that there would be a recoil from what had become an extreme. And of course there is reason to anticipate that the recoil will also flirt with extremity, until balance is restored—when it can then again fight for its life among the querulous and obtuse, who love nothing more than a skirmish.

The so-called natural-wine community is a conspicuous example of this new "popular-kid" style of wine. Perhaps the zenith of the recoil against steroid wines, it bears its own examination, which is coming right up. Like the "cool-kid" style that came before it, it is often lovely, yet its extreme examples can be seriously repulsive. Some people (like me) like "cool" flavored wines; we look for freshness, grace, and a certain quiet even when our wines are animated, because they don't yell or thrust their attributes in our faces. Other people like more extravagant wines, which they feel to be magnificent with bravura flavor and redolent of spectacle. (It's invidious to name names here; these wines are ubiquitous and can usually be located by looking for high scores in the commercial wine magazines.) I find that taste to be coarse, but it isn't morally wrong. But whew, you should hear it yowl when it defends its hegemony: *There shall be no other gods before me, no popular kids but* us.

The prevalent recoil from the bruiser wine idiom has corresponded with a new generation of wine drinkers, many of whom are smarter than me and my grizzled peers. Yet millennials, as they are called, make their own mistakes, often seeming to approach wine as a vast horizontal plane where everything is equally valid and there are no orders of salience. And they seem to be eager for novelty. By contrast, when I was starting out in wine, I wanted to lay its organizing principles in some sort of architecture of importance, and so I had to know the classics. Today the young drinker can't afford the classics, and also thinks they're boring.

When my geezer wine pals get together, it isn't long before we're bemoaning the state of play among these feckless youngsters. *You kids amuse yourselves with your crappy little wines with no fruit and too much acidity and your bizarre nerdy flavors*—alas, too often this dismay is justified—*and you just go on pretending you're popular but you're* not; *you're just a bunch of ignorant drips who couldn't fit in with* cool *people.*

It feels good to vent, but this is also when I get squirrely. Any sentence beginning "These young people . . ." or "People today . . ." is extremely likely to devolve into truism and bromide. I actually find young wine drinkers to be amazing and wonderful—often wrong, but always kinetic. And besides, it's our job to be wrong in our twenties. And to emerge from wrongness is preferable to always having been right, since it means you're still learning. If these folks are too fond of novelty, so what? The next generation will swing back over to the anchors and benchmarks, and the millennials will bemoan their callow descendants: *For this we threw open the doors for you? So you could obsess over Bordeaux and Burgundy?*

As I write, the old popular-kid style of wine seems to be concluding and the newer one seems to be nascent, and the result is a kind of cacophony, which isn't a bad thing. Obviously not all of those popular-kid wines of the 1990s and early 2000s were grotesque, but some of them were, and they were singled out for effusive and fulsome praise in certain quarters, until the market answered with a collective *meh*. Then the equal and opposite reaction took place, as could have been predicted, and while that current was both healthy and necessary, it also gave rise to some wines that were more grotesque than the old styles we eschewed. As could have been predicted!

To produce more moderate wines is a struggle against the tendencies of a warming planet. Even if you don't agree that too many of the wines produced in the past few decades taste overripe, you will have to agree that climate change is having a giant impact on the way wines taste. Then we start to ask questions like, What impact? Is this a good thing? Is it worrisome? Is it both good and worrisome?

In the latter decades of the twentieth century, quality-minded vintners did everything they could to maximize the potential for ripeness. They had to. The weather, often too cold, was a fickle friend. And so they planted on the sunniest slopes and in the warmest places; they lowered their yields so that the vines would direct their strength toward ripening a smaller quantity of fruit. They started making multiple passes through their vineyards at harvest time, each time in search of the ripest grapes. They picked as late as they dared. As the climate warmed, at first they were euphoric — one fine vintage after another! Yet as the years went along, the growers sometimes found their wines fatiguing and overstated. All their hard work and passion were in effect being punished by nature, by the new omnipresent warmth.

But it can't all be blamed on climate, because other factors were also in play. One was the ever-increasing tendency toward organic and biodynamic grape-growing, and many of the "natural" sensibilities of which these were a part. Fermenting with so-called wild (or ambient, or natural) yeast came into play. But this was at first incompletely understood, and some wines had sluggish fermentations that didn't always complete. This could result in wines that were high in alcohol and contained residual sugar. These viscous puddles of ripeness were no one's idea of fun. At the same time an idea took ever-greater hold on the zeitgeist: that of what was called physiological ripeness, aka phenolic ripeness, the state at which phenols are ripe enough to be palatable. (Phenols in white wine are analogous to tannin in red: if they're not ripe, they taste puckery and astringent.) No longer did it suffice to pick by sugar alone; you had to have "ripe" seeds and sweet-tasting skins, which usually meant waiting even longer to pick. And all of this made perfect sense—except that the weather kept getting warmer. And in many years the decision to await physiological ripeness meant wines with well over 14 percent final alcohol. (At times over 15 percent and even 16 percent, from especially hot climates.)

Each of these new paradigms was virtuous. Lowering yields would give more concentrated wines. Organic viticulture was good for the world. Understanding true ripeness would bring more deliciousness to the glass. Yet a capricious and ever-warming climate threatened to bring the whole edifice crashing down. Indeed, some regions (notably Alsace) experienced a market torpor that has led to an identity crisis that in turn is leading to many fervid questions: How do we escape from this? And, even more fundamental, what do we conceive wine to *be*?

Wine, self-evidently, can be many things and many ways, from teensy little Vinho Verde or those miniature miracles of Moscato d'Asti, up through German Rieslings (with some residual sugar) and their 7.5–10 percent alcohol, up through Champagne with its 12–12.5 percent, and then perhaps to the biggest bump in the schemata, all those ripe dry wines around 13.5 percent. And then to the grotesqueries, the bruiser wines that some people relish and I can't abide. I think we agree: lots of different kinds of wines. I think we'd also agree that the question of what we conceive wine to *be,* or of how we wish it to be, depends on our own tastes and preferences. Again, these are bromides.

I wonder if we would concur that wine, in its fundamental nature, is a beverage of moderate alcohol in the overall scheme of things. Only beer (and not all beer) is lighter, whereas most other alcoholic beverages are stronger. Can we unite on that? And if so, can we reach a consensus that most wine is destined for use as a table beverage to go with our meals? And if we accept that premise, would it not follow that wine should therefore be a drink that's in some way refreshing?

The question of inebriation also comes into play. Wine is an inebriant, as all alcohol is. Yet it is rather an inefficient one. Beer goes down more easily (and also quenches thirst), and spirits will get you wasted in a hurry, so for most people, if it's drunkenness they seek, there are superior alternatives to wine.

I happen to be a man who doesn't enjoy being buzzed, and so my goal is to drink more and stay as sober as possible. For me wine is essentially a beverage of moderate alcohol whose prime function (in terms of utility) is to be drunk with food, and it should be refreshing. Its alcoholic content is thus a fellow traveler that's sometimes a nuisance.

High-alcohol wines are, within this paradigm, a sort of distortion or perversion of wine's basic everyday purpose. These wines are also a threat to the innate friendliness of wine, and even if we don't decry such wines, we do well to abjure them. They are in a basic way uncivil. Even if they can't help it, they don't play well with others. The hardcore wine community might not mind this, but then again, they/we are prima facie daft and approach wine for any number of arcane purposes. The rest of us are best off if wine is one of those not-too-demanding friends.

Moderate-alcohol wines offer a large number of collateral benefits beyond those to your beleaguered liver. As a rule they result from long growing seasons and slow-ripening grape varieties. This gives nuance and complexity and articulation to their flavors. Such wines are often clear, crisply defined, transparent, and animated. They are more *interesting* than most bigger wines. They constitute the prerequisite, I think, for the emotional and spiritual experiences about which I froth and spume all over these pages. So when I force some poor sommelier to sulk away to get another bottle because the one he brought me was 14 percent alcohol or higher, maybe I'm not such a pill after all. (Or maybe I am, but for any of a hundred other reasons.) I'm looking for maximum flavor with minimal alcohol, and still, even in this challenged world, finding it. It takes some insisting, but it's worth doing.

Another vector into this discussion is to consider the value of *expressive* flavor, by which one means, most of the time, assertive flavor. "Expressive" is one of those metaphorical wine words that's entirely accurate yet incomprehensible to civilians. I can only ask you to consider the concept as it's displayed in acting, playing music, reading aloud. An expressive wine is one that has definite (and interesting) flavor and articulates it distinctly. Whereas an "assertive" wine is like an assertive person: it clamors for your attention. Big alcohol is part of this, but not the only part. When we examine the question closely, we see another example of good deeds being punished.

Here's an example. A German wine estate I worked with was called Schmitt-Wagner, located along the Mosel in the village of Longuich. It was something of a vinous heritage site, as it entailed some 6,300 very old ungrafted vines planted in 1896 and another 3,000 planted in 1903, all on steep land in a fine terroir. But Bruno Schmitt had no heirs willing to take it over, and when he became too old (in his eighties) to manage all the taxing hand labor, he looked for a buyer. To my great good fortune, he was able to sell the estate to another winery with whom I worked, Carl Loewen, just down the river in Leiwen. Karl-Josef Loewen knew very well the legacy value of the Schmitt-Wagner estate. It would be in the best possible hands.

As indeed it was and still is. By any reasonable measure, the wines have improved. But—what do we mean by "improved"? They have become more vigorous, more emphatic, and more insistent—in short, more *assertive*. My professional palate recognizes and appreciates this, and it is the way of the modern marketplace: your wine needs to make an impression, to be impressive. That's how it gets noticed, evaluated, scored, and selected from the herd for special acclaim. Much of the wine-drinking community has self-selected for geekiness (or for connoisseurship, if you'd rather), and they want to be led to the most dynamic hooch.

There is nothing at all wrong with this, and the Loewens are making splendid wine and doing full credit to Bruno's lifework. Yet I have a feeling they will agree with me that something has been lost.

I would describe this quality as a kind of tactfulness. Bruno's wines, when you taste them next to the fervid wines being made now, are gentler, less overt, more analog, more companionable, because they draw only so much attention to themselves. Theirs is a quiet purpose: to make you feel better without your noticing. These demure and soft-spoken beings can be the best kind of company, and something in our world is quashing them. It can't be blamed on weather. It can, though, be blamed on us, because we are unaware that we're asking wine to put on a show, while it seeks only to make friends. Or sought, because these kinds of wines are vanishing. Think about what they take with them into oblivion! Modesty, discretion, thoughtfulness, transparent lapidary flavors, tenderness of tone . . . and even more, the sense that a wine is simply happening, as though it were ordained to come into being in just that very way.

I find any number of things to be interesting and admirable in some wines, and sometimes these can be elevated to an exalted degree. But when I'm just drinking like any other wine-lovin' slob, I find I draw toward deliciousness, charm, and companionability.

I am ever more aware of this split in my approach to wine between what I evaluate and what I thirst for—and I don't think I'm alone. I saw this same tension at work when I visited one of my red-wine Austrian growers one year. Reinhold Krutzler is one of the Big Names in Austrian red wine. He belongs to the elite. His Perwolff is iconic. And for a long time I felt his wines were somewhat earnest, self-serious, groping to realize the stature conferred upon them and mindful of the international palates that would taste and judge them. They were polished, and at their best they tasted important, but just as often they were brooding, tannic, and disconcerting, the tannin behaving like a bouncer who wouldn't let you into the club.

There was no reason for Krutzler to change course. He was successful. And yet he did. In 2014, when I tasted a deliriously expressive new vintage of his basic Blaufränkisch, a variety that can be brooding unless it is vinified to encourage its berried lushness to come to the fore, I had to ask, "Is this the vintage, or did you make some changes in the cellar?" And he replied that he wanted more pure fruit in his wines, and to make wines that would engage the drinker and not just impress the critics. This makes me incredibly happy. It is such a kind, almost moral thing for him to have done. I have often suspected that deliberately "difficult" wines are more about the grower's ego than the drinker's happiness. You can do anything you like, offer any angles, edges, intricacies, challenges, and mysteries, if you have earned your way in by offering sensual pleasure. Give me something my body enjoys and I will follow you anywhere. But give me something my body finds opaque or repellant and I don't care what else you want to show me: I'm checked out.

The question is whether craftsmanship, intelligence, and charm are things we value enough to pay for—to pay anything for. We pay for "greatness" and we pay for "value," but when we buy a wine like this Krutzler I would argue we're paying for a kind of humanity and civility. Do you value good conversation? Then what would you say if someone observed, *What's the fuss? All you did was sit and talk.* You'd say, *You don't understand, clearly,* and you'd be correct. And you'd start to know why I feel that some wines are less cherished than they ought to be.

It's all well and good for anyone to extol wines enacting the deeper values, or what I happen to call "the deeper values," because these cannot be tasted individually but only inferred by someone who's sensitive in ways conducive to an appreciation of refinement. (This can be learned, but most often it arises over time and repeated exposure.) Nor are these values morally self-evident. They indicate an aesthetic choice. And yet I'd argue that they improve the world.

An object of keen, intense beauty can make us flush with exquisite pleasure, and perhaps while we are in that flush we're connected with a gratitude that brings us perspective and enriches our humanity. But what of the object of *modest* beauty, of small beauty, of delicate beauty? My friend Johannes Selbach (of the Mosel estate Selbach-Oster) says he wants to make wines for people to drink, as opposed to wines for him to win kudos and medals. What a curious thing to do! It flies in the face of some apparent need for humans to establish competition in anything we encounter (the ten best pictures of grasshoppers!) and appears to prefer to drift lazily along the stream of our ordinary lives. And yet Selbach's wines are never languid or indolent; they simply have a purpose more crucial than to preen for your palate. There is never remotely anything—*anything*—contrived or pimped up about a Selbach wine. "Honest" doesn't begin to do them justice; they are more than honest, they are *true*.

Anyone can erect a building with spires and gargoyles and gables and all manner of architectural flourishes, but Selbachs build a house with a foundation going deep, deep below the ground, and this we never see with our eyes, we can only infer it with something we apprehend at a level deeper than "palate." It is the taste of things that do not change and are not relative —the taste of permanence.

Showy wines can be entertaining, and they can even be ravishing, but they are putting on a show for you, sometimes a mindless show and sometimes a fine one, but they seldom do more than skate over the surface of your entire life, your life of friends and lovers and babies and dogs and leaves and birds. The inferential wine, though, meets you somewhere further below, where you actually live, sometimes in peace and sometimes in grief, sometimes in bliss and sometimes in difficulty, but always connected to all of you, not only to the you who passively observes experience.

And so the question of alcohol isn't merely the question of alcohol. The essential questions might be: Do we want all that clamor? Haven't we already got a surfeit of noise? Can wine get our attention without yawping for it? Finally, it is another, more subtle question: For what do we go to wine, entertainment or repose?

6
BOTTLE AND SOUL

I have argued that authentic, honest wines, which are the only wines that have any fundamental worth, are also the only wines that can move us. Whether any given wine is stirring depends on the way it happens to taste and on our own sensitivities—mystical, emotional, spiritual. Our individuality colors our response. Even the sensualist is more than merely sensual, because sensual delight can also ignite emotion. And many observers of wine have preferences about how they want the wine world to look. Ever-growing numbers of wine drinkers are thirsty for honesty and purity, and the mischief arises only when they think they've found it but it isn't there. And while I am always pleased to see "soul" adduced as a value, I find soul to be rather a delicate being, and I wince to see it applied to many dubious wines as though one is painting a wall with a roller.

It's time to consider the most conspicuous wave in the wine world, usually described as "natural"—though many adherents of the underlying philosophy are uncomfortable with that coinage, finding it too broad and nebulous. It's rather become topic A, in part because there are provocateurs on both sides of the line, and also because the laudable values of the "natural" community are sometimes played false by a bunch of seriously dubious wines.

It can seem, at least hypothetically, that "natural" would draw close to "soulful," but the truth is more ambiguous.

I have cast some aspersions on the natural-wine community, but one thing we share is a strong preference for soulful wines. Alas, we often mean different things by "soulful." My definition is probably too vague for members of that community, and theirs is often too rigid for me. I think soul plays not by our rules but by its own, and one of its games is to appear in disguise. This may be why, for all that I amuse myself by assuming I'm a kind of soul savant, I'm still surprised every time it shows up.

I often make the mistake, as we all do, of confusing soul with emotion. In terms of wine, we seem to infer the presence of soul when a wine is *redolent,* when it has atmospheres of non-wine things, when it echoes, peals, plays overtones. And again, in terms of wine qua wine, we usually sense the presence of soul in wines with a lot of tertiary elements—that is, things other than the clear flavors of the grapes. That's natural; soul is usually more inferential than literal.

I am talking strictly about white wines here. Reds have a different cast of characters.

How does this apply to natural wines? I feel frustrated when I see politics creeping into the question of what kinds of wines are soulful. I applaud anyone who values soulfulness in wine, but I started to wonder whether the notion of soul was being seen through a distorted prism. Let me elaborate.

To define some terms: "oxygenated" winemaking is that which exposes the developing wine to oxygen so as to encourage the early formation of tertiary flavors, those beyond the grape. Such wines carry rich image-tones, and they often show beauty in a way that seems to envelop the world in a grateful embrace, as if nothing is beyond their grasp. I love such wines, as you know. I can almost feel them flinging my imagination out into the ether.

In contrast, "reductive" winemaking begins by assuming that the grape, when it is picked, has all the flavor it can possibly have, and that winemaking must above all preserve and guard this primal vital energy. This Weltanschauung presumes that neither expense nor energy is spared in the vineyard, so that the fruit will be superb. Then you gather it and do next to nothing in the cellar. "We watch over, we guide, we protect, but we do not alter" was a kind of catechism often repeated by the greatest ever proponent of this approach, Hans-Günter Schwarz (whom you have already met, as he is a hero to me). Rather than directing your imagination outward, as oxidative wines do, these reductive wines plunge us inward, because at their best they show flavors we supposed we'd never glimpse, flavors we thought might be impossible. Our minds expand implosively, trying (often fruitlessly) to fathom and interpret the riotous signals these wines are sending. No small number of writers and drinkers have used metaphors of hallucination to depict this state.

Until recently I never felt the need to defend this category of wines. They existed quite peacefully along with their more redolent, oxygenated cousins, and the lucky drinker could only be grateful for all the many ways in which wine can be wonderful. Sadly, this seems to be changing. We're distressingly busy ginning up value judgments about red-state and blue-state wines and which ones we ought to approve of in order to be the highly ethical persons we presume we are. What a pity, to shrink the world to fit within our fatuous conceits.

A person might be troubled by reductive wines because they are made possible by virtue of recent technology. In most instances the grapes are babied in stainless steel vessels to ferment, sometimes with—*gulp*—cultured yeast and often at very cold temperatures, which in turn are created by cooling technology. The goal, remember, is to preserve the flavor in the grape, to lose as little as possible, to create explosive aromas, and the result, when the stars align, are impossibly vivid wines with scalpel-etched precision and digital clarity. Everything seems to be heightened—fruit, florality, minerality; the wines are often spritzy on the tongue, and the sensible drinker has no choice but to surrender: *WTF just hit me?*

A certain type of purist will recoil from stainless steel, from chilling technology; these people will feel such wines to be clinical, too perfect, too hermetic. And for all the superlative wines made in this idiom, there are admittedly plenty of facile hack wines, formulaic, imitating the superficial exteriors of better wines (and often taking dubious shortcuts in the process) and hoping the drinker can't tell.

One day I was screening samples from several Austrian growers for inclusion in my portfolio. As it happened, all the wines were of the reductive type. They began to feel *plausible,* paint-by-numbers; they started to seem mundane. I paused and thought about it. There was a prevailing competence that I could admire. There was a helpful attitude toward the drinker; the wines were clear, refreshing, honest—they did the job. None of them showed the air-freshener aromas of bogus enzymes and so-called perfume yeasts. Sometimes reductive wines can go too far and can taste constricted, not so much a wine as a *theory* of a wine. But not this group; all of them were good. "Good."

But one of them was much, much better than good. One guy's wines were like the difference between smiling only with your mouth and smiling with your entire face. This was Mr. Bernhard Ecker's wine: "modern" wine at its best. It is neither clinical nor denuded of life force. I love the exceptional clarity, the high-def obsessive nuance, the vital freshness, the charm and deliciousness, something of great good humor that catapults the wine above mere correctness. I don't want all wines to be as modern as these are, but I want all *modern* wines to have the soul I taste here.

Soul? Really? Well, permit me to ask a subversive question: why the hell not? Can anyone be categorically certain that soul is ineluctably absent from cultured-yeast, cold-fermented, stainless steel wine? I share the love and approval for natural wines —most of them, at least—but soul is more complex than we think, and it lives where it lives, not where we assume it lives.

I sit tasting Ecker's wines, suffused with pleasure, and find my-self wondering, *Who would reject these wines out of hand, on what principle, and to what end?* I feel acutely sad that a person would exclude herself from this form of happiness. There is no dichotomy between wines like these and the particular syntax of natural wines unless we insist there is. And if we do, we're excluding another valid species of beauty for reasons I don't think stand up.

I find soul in these wines because something in them ignites something in me. I taste plenty of modern ordinary wine that performs as needed and leaves nothing in its wake. Not these. Delight lives in these. There's also immense clarity, always a welcome value. Pure fruit and mineral density and thirst-induc-ing fragrance are all positive values. There's nothing contrived or plausible about such wines, and even "such wines" is mis-leading, because there are *very* few such wines.

Maybe it just isn't smart to assume that only tertiary vinous (as opposed to fruity) wines can ever be natural or have life force. I love them as much as I love any good wine, but it takes a different and special kind of passion to want the drinker to see virginal fruit and terroir so brilliantly. Soul, I think, is some-thing that opens and dilates, and if we insist that wines like Eck-er's are clinical, then we're closing off an avenue of bliss, and our souls are wounded. Can't an unambiguous delight also be a vector for soulfulness?

Readers in the future—assuming timorously that these words actually are read in the future—may find it quaint that we drew battle lines between types of wines. But fair is fair; some of our value judgments are legitimate and are badly needed. The world was overstuffed with icky steroidal bruiser wines—and yo, if "icky" is *not* the pluperfect subjunctive of "oaky," then it ought to be—and the revulsive spasm came not a minute too soon. The problem, as I've said, is typical of move-ments: they have to go too far to learn where they ought to have stopped. Yet natural wines comprise a laudable citizenry of the wine world, which they've made a more wholesome and civilized place. Mostly.

One night not long ago I had a wine that made me sad, and not in a good way. I won't say what it was or who made it, because there's no need to gratuitously insult the bottle or the guy; it was merely a somber example of a movement which could use a dose of self-reflection if that luckless wine was typical.

This miserable being in my glass was barely three years old, yet the color was already a dull bronze. It smelled like camphor, wet dog, and naphthalene (mothballs), yet each time I thought, *This wine is unsound,* I heard some young wine lover admonish me to stop being such a techno-dweeb, insisting that these were terroir aromas (they are not) and soulful aromas (only if your soul is a badly damaged place) and natural aromas (yes, just like the mildew smell of a shower curtain that needs to be cleaned), and when thought and language are thus corrupted it makes me feel a kind of grief. I almost found myself yearning for the steroidal ick-wine.

I like most natural wines and most of the people who make them, and the movement deserves better than the wine I was drinking. It needs a few wise elders to police the perimeter and remind people that flawed wine isn't some noble-savage form of atavism—it's just flawed wine, no more virtuous than body odor.

I hoped that wine would taste better than it smelled. I decanted it (as they say you should; I'm an obedient guy), and I really tried to like it, because a person should be open-minded. I was nearly ready to go on and drink the bottle, taking one for the team, when I noticed my mouth starting to hurt from the wine's gritty tannin. Nor was I happy with the bitter alcoholic (14.5 percent) finish, which reminded me why kids scream when you make them swallow medicine.

It then struck me that I've had a lot of wines like this, and that wines in a certain subgenre (I hope it's a *sub*genre) of the natural-wine community are prone to be quite a bit alike. And even sadder, that they taste as generic as the wines they correctly are rebelling against. The way such wines are made is hardly less formulaic than the way the dreadful bruiser wines were made; it's just that we approve of this formula; we wrap it in raiments of feel-goody values. The *values* are just fine, as long as the wines are drinkable. If I were any sort of mouthpiece for this movement — about as likely as finding two identical snowflakes, but work with me — I'd guard those values by protecting them from yucky wines. Excellent and beautiful wines grow out of the natural sensibility, honoring the sensibility and embodying the values. Those kinds of wines are completely convincing because when a wine is that beautiful, we infer that its underlying values must also be beautiful.

Imagine that I was trying to make a case for wine from "fully ripe fruit," and let's say the wine I chose to make my point with was one of those cartoonlike critters with 16 percent alcohol and the taste of prunes having nightmares. I'd be using the worst possible wine to make my point. Thus I cringe to drink a wine as nasty and rustic — and, by the way, chemical-tasting — as that melancholy night's wine. The movement, community, call it what you wish, deserves better. And bad wine goes on being bad wine.

I understand that I have created two reductios ad absurdum, though neither example is actually absurd, because both of them exist. The worst of the modern reductive wines are merely contrived and tedious. We are safe to ignore them. The worst of the old-school oxygenated wines, though, are acutely nasty and objectionable, and one wishes they were easier to ignore.

All the while, in the golden mean all manner of gladness is there to be found. And at this point soul puts in an appearance, because it needs to complain about being corrupted by the acutely dirty wines that sometimes appear under the natural-wine banner, which lay specious claim to soulfulness as a means of justifying how yucky they taste. I am no Guardianof-Soul, but I know enough to know that soul wants no part of wines that smell like dung heaps.

What, then, may we suppose soul does want? Is it even possible? Or does it succumb to the inevitable vagueness that enters into talks about soul?

Maybe you have to sneak up on it. Whisper in its ear from behind. (In fact whispering is inherently soulful, I think, which is why babies like it.) In many tertiary natural wines there are qualities of gentleness and inference, which can still our hearts and rouse us to reverie. Daydreaming is always soulful. Scent arouses memory and memory makes us pensive. The direct modern wine, in contrast, is like lifting the lid on the soup and inhaling deeply; the indirect wine is like coming home to the house where the soup is cooking. One is the smell of food, the other is the smell of home. So yes, the tertiary wines are things of atmosphere, flowing outward into the larger sensual world. But thinking isn't always soulful. Even imagining or remembering isn't always soulful. Receiving a gesture of tenderness, as one often does from a redolent wine of low or moderate alcohol, is intensely stirring but not invariably soulful. Falling through the trapdoor into the peak experience is a kind of bathing in soul, but it arrives capriciously.

In fact, soul never arrives when it is summoned. How many times has the grand bottle let you down? How many times has the great occasion not really been all that great? How many times have you finally gotten that promotion you worked your ass off for and wondered why you don't feel happier? Maybe this is just some quirk of mine; I can't seem to celebrate on command. And so I enact a facsimile of the expected emotion, and meanwhile an emptiness grows. The next day I'm alone in my kitchen, and I see an ordinary sparrow stepping carefully in the new snow on our deck, and then soul shows up, but of course my timer goes off and the tea is ready and has to come off the leaves. It's a green tea, and it smells like warm grass, and it's lovely to drink it while I look at the new snow out my window, and for an instant I delight in the contrast of warm grass and cold snow — but is it soulful? It's just a moment I noticed.

If you drink a bottle from a grower you know personally, if you have visited or maybe even made friends, the wine of course is larger and richer, no longer an object but a being that lives among the filaments of your recollection, and that is wonderful and many-dimensional. But I'm not sure it's soulful.

Back when my wife and I were in our early courtship, we were long-distance, and there were times we couldn't bear to go apart, and so we changed my flight or hers and stole a twenty-four-hour reprieve. This called for Champagne. What love and relief attended the drinking of that first glass! But now I think of the day after, when the inevitable could no longer be delayed, we staged our infinitely tragic goodbye at the airport, and I returned home to the silence. Oh, the terrible spaces in that air; I hope never to know them again. There was sometimes a bottle in the fridge, the Champagne we didn't finish. I'd pour myself a glass, listening to the crackle of the mousse in the unnervingly quiet kitchen. When I think of those lonely glasses of Champagne from the bottle we couldn't finish before we parted, *that* is soulful. Her ghost glides around the room, the sandwich she made but only ate half of is sitting in the fridge, the bed is creased from the weight of her body. Later in the night I'll find a sock under the covers; she kicks them off after her feet are warm. But now it's just me and a sad glass of Champagne.

Drinking a very old wine can be a soulful experience, and — at least for me — it is almost always an experience of love, gratefulness, and sadness. Soul indeed seems in some way to adhere to sadness. Not that it *is* sad, but it rides on the back of sadness like a little kid on his dad's shoulders.

Soul also likes to wear inexplicable garments, likes to speak in riddles, likes to cultivate ambiguity, always feels the same but never looks the same, and seems to like to have you to itself. That might be my introversion talking, but when I feel a moment of soul it removes me from my environment. Thus I don't equate it with awe or even with love. Soul is a dark meaning, and the longer I live, the more the maps dissolve, and while I do feel that wines can be soulful, and I do feel that certain things encourage a wine to be soulful, this can be neither scripted nor known. Just be there when it whispers.

If there is a reliable marker for soul—*if*—then perhaps it is depth. The very word "depth" suggests the unseen, the subterranean. Wines of depth aren't always pretty. And I actually believe that wines of depth are marked by their serene indifference to how we happen to feel about them. They have a larger purpose than to entertain my smug self. They have no need at all to show how quirky they are, how atavistic, how original, how meaningful. Meaningful is what one is, not what one displays. Wines of depth are engaged in an obscure business, yet it's from just those very fogs that soul can appear, whispering, daring to find you and make you sad.

I find the moment of soul makes me not larger but smaller. It whispers to little me. It makes me feel like I'm standing on a small hill, in all my littleness, suddenly looking at a larger view, stretching to my entire tiny height, failing to understand what I see, yet belonging somehow, and oddly and completely alone.

In writing about soul, or the thing I call soul, I find much of that writing is like soul itself is: inexplicable and unnervingly close to gibberish. At least mine is. I'm insecure about that writing—people will think it vapid—and I'm also strangely proud of it—at least I tried.

I also like to write about what I call the mystical, and this can be conflated with soul, but I don't think they are the same. They sometimes ride together in the same vehicle of a person's temperament, and perhaps they are relatives, but nothing more. Wine, I find, can offer soulful moments (as I have written and written and *written* about), but it also is a vector to mystical (or peak) experience. One reliable phenomenon is the experience of inexplicable paradox. When a wine offers flavors or textures that seem as though they'd be mutually exclusive, I am amazed, and wonder is only a breath away—and the mystical only another breath away from that. Paradox has a fellow traveler: ambiguity, the sense that something is neither this nor that at the same time that it is *both* this and that.

There is a trick that composers know. In essence, you superimpose two chords, one enmeshed with the other. That creates an ambiguous key center. The listener's mind seeks to organize the input into something definite, and it is thwarted, delightfully (for someone like me) or frustratingly (for some alien kind of person). The composer Michael McGlynn, who writes for his choral group Anúna, is a master at this effect, and when he combines close-together tonalities and these dual chords are sung by women, the effect can be a kind of weightlessness, a suspension of definition that feels like freedom, release, liberation from the categorical world.

When the mind is thus confounded, it moves urgently back and forth to locate an organizing principle; when that isn't found, one either retreats or surrenders. I have found that a dislocated mind will often stumble through the portal to mystical experience. Apart from the musical world, I suspect that anything hurling the mind about as it seeks to determine this-or-that is handing us a key. I think now of the experiences of ambiguity—"It is doubtful whether we are this or that or some blend of both"—and also ambivalence—"I feel both this way and that way and there is a dissonance involved because both things cannot be true at once"—that leave the mind unmoored, at which point a glimmer may be sensed. In any case, I find it beautiful, whether in music or in literature or indeed in life. In the world of beauty, indefinition is inherently wonderful. It usually describes a kind of grave yet lovely struggle, to come to terms with whatever doubt is residing with you.

With wine I find these unmoored moments in "both-and" flavors, when the mind is confronted with ostensibly impossible combinations—creaminess with backbone, or gloss with power, or, to go further into metaphor, fervor with tenderness. When I write the word "yet" in a tasting note, I know I'm onto some-thing and the wine is special. The coexistence of the mutually exclusive calls everything into question, as these elements are compatible after all. Here's something I didn't know! What else don't I know? What does this new thing say about the world?

This can happen with young wines, but rarely, as they often show a definite youthful energy and fruit. Still, it can happen, and most often those wines hail from masters of texture, peo-ple like Raveneau, Alzinger, Dönnhoff, where the most fastidi-ously detailed nuances of flavor are seen through a kind of ten-der gauze. I once wrote, "Drinking this wine is like having your temples massaged while you look into a microscope."

With old wines the paths are clearer. The wines are more inferential, more polytonal, more (if you will) ambiguous, and they show us something about complexity: that it is different from intricacy, that it has to do with things that cannot be seen or known, that it isn't just a complicated design but an opening into the inscrutable.

Here was a wine that shows what I'm trying to say. It arrived to be tasted blind, which was fine, as it wasn't any sort of a con-test. We were in Champagne, and we assumed that it would be a Champagne. The cork was bad and there wasn't much mousse remaining, but the golden-hued wine exhaled the most gorgeous old-wine fragrance, sea-deep, nutty, wildly herbal and curiously *sweet,* and that was the first dissociative moment, the gravitas of the aroma with the dancing beaming sweetness on the palate.

It became a meaning-of-life wine, this lovely strange old be-ing. The merest surmise of bead, a stray little bubble drifting up to the surface every few seconds, a little crackle on the tongue. It started to smell like really, really fresh farm chicken . . . but then I stopped writing what it smelled like. It didn't matter. The wine was too mysterious; the minty finish above the umber-evening aroma above the still-energetic palate seemed a kind of encom-passing, as if it remembered, knew, or anticipated an entire lifetime. The high sweetness held the wine's energy, but it seemed to want to tread toward gravity, dignity, and sadness.

It was in fact a 1933, probably the sweet style called demi-sec (at least). It started showing an almost arch saltiness. My god, what to make of this wine? It started to taste almost like wintergreen, it was like chewing elderblossom. It decoupled the mind from its judging and identifying functions, and I flew up toward the ceiling like a birthday balloon.

The world isn't quite what we think it is, ever. This strange sad gorgeous wine will die in its sleep, painlessly, and all its accounts will have been settled. For a moment it didn't matter that the bottle was generously shared by a friend, that it entailed a sentimental history for him, or that all of us were amazed by it. A wine like this one just erases the world, even as it encompasses the world, even as it sends a depth probe into some ocean floor of the spirit.

Laughter and joy are contagious, but the moment of beauty is—at least for me—a pure silence, an utter solitude. While it is occurring it cannot be shared.

There's a line in the sleeve notes to one of Robert Fripp's Soundscape records that says, "Silence is our friend." Our absurd friend, perhaps, since the sentiment would seem to obviate the need for music, or even the voice that reads the line. But that's what's so nice about writing. I do it in silence and you read it in silence.

But what is the silence we speak of? There's the poetic silence, which is desirable, and the actual silence, which is unnerving. Absolute pure silence is a sort of violence, especially if one's inner landscape is unquiet. Very often silence is associated with loneliness or sorrow. If you take your loved one to the airport and you kiss at the curb and you watch her walk into the terminal, there's nothing like the moment when you get back home and open the door to an empty house. If you're tempted to claim that silence is my friend just then, I'd rather you didn't.

Yet there is a craving, if not for silence, then at least for the noise to stop. Drinking any good wine can concentrate one's attention into a fine slim filament that links the wine to you and you to the wine, and for that small moment the noise goes away. If the wine is tender, allusive, or profound, it really banishes all the chaos, not just in that very moment but as long as it echoes and peals.

And then of course we swallow it. We absorb it into our bodies. We may experience this silence with art or music or literature, but looking, listening, and reading are different from swallowing. The silence plays on, and the wine is mixing with our very blood. I like to talk about wine, but I don't like being compelled to, and lately I've taken a geezer's privilege and just talked about the wine in its moment. Sometimes that entails a discussion of its flavors, but only when these pertain to the moment. I'm starting to insist that it's proper to ask, *Just what's happening now? It's so tough to hold it all still, but what are you thinking, what are you feeling, what are you envisioning, imagining, receiving?* There is a world within that silence. Nothing lives in it, but everything visits, arriving and fading, flashing and vanishing.

7

SERVING THE THIRSTY GHOST

I distinguish between wines made since I started drinking wine and wines made before that time. If it's a vintage I knew when it was young, in some stubborn way it remains young. It's like looking at an adult you knew as a baby; you always see the newborn. This feckless adult who stands before you is a kind of trick, a chimera. So if I drink a 1971, it isn't an old wine even if it tastes like one. You might observe that this is just me in denial about aging, but I'm not denying anything. I'm *happy* to be aging. The alternative is too unsettling. It is, rather, a curious palimpsest having to do with the nature of memory and the curvings of time.

When I drink a wine that predates my wine discovery, that is an old wine. And it is unfathomable. What does the date on the label mean? What can it mean? If you do the math and the wine is seventy years old or whatever, how viscerally real is that at the moment of tasting? Over the years I have come to expect that old wines will be *interior* in a way that young wines seldom are, and more sedate. But I do not—cannot—approach such wines expecting my soul to be shaken. Indeed, approaching any experience expecting one's soul to be shaken is a recipe for disappointment. While the repose and complexity of old wines often induce reverie, the appearance of soul is whimsical and capricious, and all you can do is to be ready and have the fireplace going.

But let's pause for a moment, to try to be more clear. When I speak of soul, I refer to an abstract or metaphysical condition from which we all borrow and with which we are all imbued. If I speak of "my" soul, I mean only the portion of the collective soul that's given to me in certain moments, and if I speak of a wine's soul, that is me inferring the presence of this phenomenon in the wine. It's like sunlight. It isn't my sunlight, though I might stand in it, and it isn't the tree's sunlight, though it falls on the tree. It's there and we all take from it.

Sometimes my soul may be shaken. If a wine tastes "old"—that is, if it tastes fragile and inscrutable and interior—then I am roused to the core by its dignity and by the soft light of its incipient demise. Alternately, if the wine tastes youthful, notwithstanding its age, that is even more ridiculously beautiful, and that kind of virtual confit of its vitality represents a courage that affirms something for which I have no name. I can't draw a logical thread between either of these experiences and the sadness that arrives with them. For me, it just does. The evening of a life is a matter of *tristesse,* and the insistent bright morning of a life caught in the teeth of time and its ravages is so poignant—all that valor in the certainty of defeat—I can only nod toward the fleeting innocent being, ruefully. Too many angels passing by unnoticed.

Not long ago a friend opened a bottle of 1971 Barolo for me, a wine about which he had some doubt. It hadn't always been stored well. It was Nebbiolo, the wine of doubts and fogs. "If it isn't good we'll open something else," he said. Opened deliberately, decanted slowly, and poured.

It started out in a state of aphasia, a chaos of tannin, acidity, and decay. And then in a few minutes there was an eerie kind of knitting into a faded vitality that completely transported me. The other three at the table agreed, but only I was launched into a fugue state. This old being, the smoke clinging to his hair and his clothes, the ancient language he spoke with such clarity and brevity, seemed to contain death and life inside a single skin. I can't remember what I must have babbled; someone else said, "Well, *Terry's* in the zone," and I confess I was riveted. In about fifteen minutes the wine rattled its way into demise, its soft mesmeric light extinguished, but while it shone it was pale but not feeble, and for those brief minutes it was impossible to be false.

I thought on the drive home, *What is the true best way to drink great wine?* Not everyday wine but *great* wine? And the answers were either alone with a notebook and pen or with one other person in a state of calm—no dinner to prep, no last train to catch, not even a conversation to maintain. And either way, at home. I've had plenty of great wines in restaurants, and many times I feel a little sad; there's so much else going on, and not enough of me.

I'm remembering, now, a bottle of sweet Amigne de Vétroz, drunk on the terrace of a hotel/restaurant in Verbier, as the alpenglow settled on the glaciers of the Grand Combin across the valley and the first stars appeared. But I *felt* alone, and, more crucially, I felt available to be absorbed into the universe; that's what great wine wants. And eventually I really *was* alone, as my wife was getting cold, even beneath the blanket the staff had thoughtfully delivered, so she went upstairs and I drank the last glass under the stars by myself, a sweet wine in a starry dark world.

If you live long enough, you make friends with a lot of ghosts. If you were adopted in the era of secret, "closed" adoptions, as I was, you walk with ghosts from your first day alive. You live astride two worlds, one of which insistently enacts its ostensible reality and the other of which shimmers around your being, just out of sight, and this second place seems entirely real, though it's peopled with specters and secrets. My adoptive parents—of course, my *parents*—were wonderful people whom I was very happy and lucky to know. I'm far from a hero of any grand tragedy. I lucked out. All kids have imaginary friends, but I had an imaginary family, an entire imaginary history. I had, even as a little kid, some sort of inchoate parallel world, and as kids are wont to do, I believed these phantoms were as real as everything I saw around me. Perhaps this is why wine seems so alive to me.

Of course a living person is preferable to any ghost or any bottle of wine, but the ghost and the wine can tell you things that the living person has no words for. I love conviviality, the warm company of sympathetic beings, and there is a sacrament in the sharing of wine with other souls. But sometimes there's a bottle so searching, sweet, and ghostly that I can't help following it off along its dark shore, alone. I've learned to apologize to my friends! "I go bye-bye, back in a bit; anyone got pen and paper?" Sometimes I try to say what I'm feeling, and then I know my friends really like me, because I'm acting rather loopy.

And sometimes the living people you long for simply aren't there, so you have to make do with ghosts and wine. As a matter of fact, the entire chain of events that led me to a life in wine might be said to have started a few weeks before I entered my senior year of high school, when, one day, my father died. I don't mean to sound flip; it was just like that—one day. He was forty-nine, it was a heart attack, I came home from my summer job and he was right in the middle of it, and then he went to the hospital and five hours later my mother came home alone.

I had turned seventeen a few days earlier. I wasn't an especially obstreperous teenager, but I was certainly as impatient, contemptuous, and self-obsessed as anyone that age. It also happened that in my particular family there were two parallel dyads: my mother and sister as one unit and then my father and me. I gave Mom a terrible time, and I wasn't all that easy on Dad, but in fact he could control me. In the moment of crux, his will was stronger than mine. My mother's was not. And so when he died I became one point of what was now a triangle, and the other two points began to retreat into an ever-growing distance. I was unmoored; no one could steer me.

This didn't happen immediately. I finished high school with decent grades. The last thing my newly widowed mother needed was for me to go nuts. I went to college according to plan. But I started to veer off the rails, and there was no force to hold me.

The basics of the story are these: I took what was intended as a break from school, moved in with my girlfriend, went to Europe, went back to Germany to revisit places I'd spent my middle-school years in (Dad worked for Voice of America and we were stationed in Munich), grew to love it there, didn't want to leave, tried nearly fruitlessly to score a gig writing about rock music, did odd jobs to keep food on the table, and then—wine.

Life seems inexorable when viewed in reverse, but I can only surmise that if my father hadn't died, I would probably have stayed in school. I'd have majored in something interesting but useless, and I can't fathom what I'd have ended up doing with my life. I doubt I'd have gone back to Germany except on a summer-backpacking trip.

Obviously there's something facile about hypothetical retrospectives. That flaccid trope about "things happening for a reason" simply isn't true. Usually things just happen, and we read in the reason when we look back later, believing that we glean some narrative pattern that brings us to now. *If* this *hadn't happened, then* that *wouldn't have happened* does not imply that this caused that, only that one thing happened and then some other thing did. What's more reasonable, perhaps, is to wonder at the serpentine paths that can lead us from misfortune to fortune.

The fact is, if my father hadn't died when he did, it's hugely unlikely I'd have found my way to wine as and when I did, and maybe not at all. Dad didn't seem to be into wine, and it wasn't part of our household. Yet I sometimes sense his ghost strolling somewhere near me, looking at my life's work in wine and saying, "Well, I'll be damned."* My dad was a cultured guy, a

---

* A curious aside: Just a few years ago I found that my father had edited a book. It told the story of his platoon during the two years the men advanced east through France and Germany near the end of World War II. It takes the form of a diary. I discovered that my father's unit had actually occupied wine villages I know quite well, in the Mittelhaardt

classic George McGovern liberal who smoked cigars and had a semimonthly poker klatsch, on which I sometimes eavesdropped. Imagine the effect on my fifteen-year-old mind, hearing the sounds of the game (and the not infrequent ribaldry) along with tangential conversations about Ingmar Bergman's latest film or whether Albee or Pinter was the greater playwright. So there was culture in the vicinity, but not wine. I was not exposed to it at all.

Yet I found my way to wine all the same. Lucky for me, because this preoccupation snaps very neatly into two sprockets of my temperament. One is the pleasure I take in beauty, and the other is the joy I take in fascination. Wine provides me with both. It is beautiful and fascinating in ways that few other things are.

It is only very recently that I realized my father, had he survived the heart attack, would probably be dead by now. I feel lighter when I think of this. For every day of my life since he died, I have walked with him. Richard Lischer puts it quite sweetly in his book *Stations of the Heart,* saying, "The dead are completed beings who are no longer subject to the limitations of time and space and are therefore available to us across the entire surface of our lives."

A comfort with ghosts can lead to a comfort with the ghostly, and many old wines straddle a delicate line between earth and spirit. One recent bottle came from my wife's birth year. She isn't old by a long shot, but the bottle was. Three of us shared it, and one person said, "Sea spray," and we all agreed. But this was one of those old Rieslings with the most delicate, inscrutable dignity. When I heard "sea spray," I could only envi-

---

area of the Pfalz. I know growers in those villages. I even buy wine from growers in those villages. And some thirty-two years before I set foot there, my dad was in those same towns and villages, leading a platoon against the retreating Nazis. If I had supernatural powers, I would plunge into the past and I'd send my dad a dream, as the old gods did to the heroes of the Greek myths, and the dream would tell him that he and his comrades had liberated those villages for the son he would someday have—for me.

sion a body walking into the surf, the water getting higher and higher—waist, chest, shoulders, neck—until the figure disappeared into the waves, enveloped, even safe, thrust back and forth by the indefinite currents, maybe not dead but *all gone,* all absorbed and included. But . . . the price is to drown.

It smelled of cellars and of "the past" and yet it was very much in the present; it had the classic Pfalz tastes—it was a 1952 Spätlese from Deidesheim—of ginger and lemon zest, but all echoey, as if heard from across a wide valley. What was at first earthy and even a little sour started to smell like a closet full of dresses, each one carrying a different scent . . . sweet grain, wild plum, the ghost-bodies who wore those garments giving their voices to the impulses we call flavors.

I can't escape the image of being taken to the edge by something that knows more about sadness and death than I do. Though the wine was firm and solid, it seemed to be coated with interstellar dust, seemed to speak with something glaucous and mournful.

We spend our wine lives considering what the glass brings to us. But how much time do we spend considering whom we bring to the glass and how this thing changes and alters as we move through our lives? My relationship to beauty (and thus to wine) is different than it was before. The contrast grows ever more vivid. I want to describe it, and to follow the thought where it leads.

The last time I reread Fitzgerald's *Tender Is the Night* it seemed to me a significantly different book than I'd apprehended in any previous reading. And it struck me: this was the first time I'd read the novel when I was older than the author when he wrote it. I'd wager that anyone who reads seriously—a pitiable sort of word to use for this visceral pleasure—has benchmark books, books we read again and again at different points in our lives. We measure our own shapes and learn our own narratives by seeing how the new us responds to a text we've read before. Some books, it turns out, really weren't all that good, and others are good in new and revealing ways, and sometimes we've long since learned the tricks that dazzled our eager young eyes. What ravished us then is rueful to us now. And, of course, what sailed right by our callow young minds becomes crucial to us in midlife.

It isn't only the grave or the solemn whose voices we learn to hear. My crush on dry Muscat is a direct result of my getting older and learning to cherish the baby's coos and gurgles. Muscat is primordial innocence in liquid form, and when I look at my rapidly graying beard in the mirror, I think of the splash of eternal youth I'll drink in a few hours. But none of this is especially original; we all know our tastes change as we move through life, and I covered that ground elsewhere. Yet the word "taste" seems too narrow, because what changes is not only what we taste but *who we are,* tasting. The part of us that used to be entertained by massive powerful wines was also at home in cacophonous restaurants, and now we're grateful for a little quiet. Simple force is a thing that palls. And this is common, maybe even blatant; we learn to cherish subtler things.

There's something below this phenomenon that I want to explore. Because when I read my old tasting notes—which I do when I'm home alone with the blinds drawn—I see the work of a young man, effulgent with his own delight, certain the world is lyrically arranged just for his very pleasure. At least he is grateful, and willing to engage. And his—my—influences were a bygone generation of wine writers who had no fear of writing extravagantly, and who encouraged me to suppose wine could be extravagantly beautiful. So I was ready—at times too ready.

Thinking back, I have to ask, what does a thirty-year-old man even make of a sixty-year-old wine, if he's lucky enough to encounter one? What can he make of it? The number is so abstract as to be absurd. For me it was an induced moment of "significance," because my reading had trained me to anticipate a Meaningful Experience, and so an old wine became an exalted entertainment over which I emoted, as seemed to be proper. I couldn't feel the elegy of a very old wine; it blew right past me. The flavors were certainly compelling, yet even then it barely registered beyond the level of an exotic and lofty specimen. One needed an older soul than the one I had then in order to hear the nocturnes those old beings were playing.

But if this was the worst of my youthful errors (alas, it wasn't), I could easily indulge it. There are worse things than seeing wine as a bringer of beauty.

One starts there. Beauty comes to us in many forms, and one of them is wine. And then one continues, I think, and the first question is, what is the "I" to whom wine comes? Because my life has been not only a succession of selves forming and fading over time but an entire and often unruly assembly of selves clamoring at once for my attention. These many selves also shape-shift and come into being and leave again, sometimes returning and other times not, and sometimes returning in different forms. Lately I've found an especially hungry homesick self whose clamor was drowned out by my excitement in traveling as a younger man. Not anymore. The part of me that still loves going away is like a very drowsy dog who needs to be cajoled into wakefulness.

I think perhaps that part of the soul's business is to gradually pare down this parliament of selves we carry through life until some true voice can be heard. It sounds a little affected to say "the soul's voice," but I can't contrive a better phrase. The young soul tries on a bunch of different voices, a whole chorus trilling away. Then fewer and fewer, because the soul knows before we ourselves do that time is drawing down, and if we're ever going to hear the pure authentic voice, we'd better listen now. I've said that if we live long enough, we walk with a lot of ghosts, but the unnerving surprise is that eventually we walk with our own. Maybe it arrives when it's summoned and maybe it was somewhere in the back of the scrum, but however it happens, part of me is walking with the Terry who won't be here forever.

What can this possibly have to do with wine? More than you may suppose. It certainly had everything to do with wine when I drank a wine of my birth year during a visit to Gaston Chiquet in Champagne.

It was a quiet Sunday and we'd just driven from Germany. My hotel's Wi-Fi was balky and it was a crisis time at the company, so I was distracted and jangly. But at least we'd be with Nicolas Chiquet, who is among my favorite people, and I knew I'd get lost in the wines. That's easy to do there.

Nicolas says he doesn't have very many visitors who love old wines, so when we arrive it's an opportunity to plunder the cellar. That makes me feel bashful. I mean, who am I to deserve this? And the cellar, after all, is finite; when those bottles are gone, they're gone.

Two wormy old bottles arrived, coated in cellar fuzz. (Your hands get all goopy if you hold a bottle like that.) The cork was stubborn in the first one, and in the moments after the wine was poured none of us could be sure it wasn't corked. Old wine sometimes starts off smelling like the cellar—that is, moldy— and it takes a minute or two to figure out which is which. The wine was from the '50s, but more than that we could not know. Nicolas thought it may have been demi-sec, which would have made it nonvintage quality; he makes demi-sec only as a non-vintage. This would imply Pinot Meunier, which is a substantial variety in his NV wines. So yes, maybe. The color was oddly fresh—further evidence of TCA (aka the taste of bad cork)— and the initial aromas were riotous until the TCA subsumed them: truffle, brown butter, tonka bean, orange zest, maple, melon, some crazy esterization of fructose, and we had a good five to ten minutes with it before we all had to agree, sadly, that the cork taste was winning the race. Still, I was grateful to visit the wine at all.

Nicolas knew what the next wine was, but I don't know if he knew it was from my birth year, 1953. It was one of his last four bottles. I was half in tears before the bottle was open, me and my little sixtieth birthday the summer before. As he eased the cork from the neck of the bottle, I felt suitably grave. Mortality, beauty, friendship; the little parlor where we tasted might as well have been a chapel.

It was a difficult time professionally, and I was anxious, a long way from myself. The man I brought to that glass was in a state of *what, me, now?* Nicolas said the cork was strong, "perfect," and the wine was poured with delicate ceremony. I sniffed it, and it took all my strength not to weep out loud. Not that I'm scared about crying in front of others, but this wine threatened to undo me. Still, my eyes filled and my voice caught, and I followed the wine into whatever silence and starlight it wanted to show me.

It smelled like every weeping buttered nut since the beginning of time. It had a four-octave complexity, a full measure of power that was virtually heroic, and the vitality of a great wine from a great vintage, in miraculous condition. I was out past the galaxy of associations; there was only an infinitely tender and mysteriously complex loveliness, a consoling sweetness in the finish that froze my heart with ecstasy and regret, as such things always do, that sweet sad message of the beauty of the world, telling me, *Try not to forget this. It's hard, I know it's hard, but you have to try.*

The room grew very quiet, four tasters with our souls eased into stillness, expanding silently and infinitely. There were murmurings in the wine, and the silence was a balm. But what I heard was unquiet. I hadn't given much credence to "turning sixty," because who knows what that's supposed to mean? I didn't feel sixty, whatever that was, and I felt no dilution of passion. A few years on I do feel certain changes in the body, asking me to be a little gentler, and I feel powerful shifts among my sources of joy, all of them asking me to spend more time at my wellsprings, the taproots and fountainheads that a young man feels he can safely ignore. I know I can't ignore them now. There's not enough time. And this dancing thing in my glass was a herald of time.

How much time do I have left? I wondered. Believe me, I'm not especially lugubrious and I'm not fixated on questions of death. But sixty, you know—you let a few of those thoughts in. You can't help it. Sitting there, drinking a wine precisely as old as I was, aware of the dark penumbra always around beauty, I asked myself if I felt ready for death. I mean in an abstract way. Ask me "Are you ready to die?" and I'll say *fuck* no, but ask, "Are you ready for death?" and I'll say, "For sure not tomorrow, but I guess eventually." But this wine wouldn't let me split that question. It knew very well how I really felt: *How can I bear to leave this world? This* world.

And what of all the days and days between these still-framed moments of stunning kindness? The days when we forget what it actually is we *do* by living. In the rapturous gravity of these exquisite flavors, I think I never want another single one of those thoughtless days. But of course I do. I want those ordinary beats of living and I want them never to stop. But I also don't want to forget the way a wine like this can light up the interior, and we need to wander down there now and again and do a census of all the strange critters who live there. They get obstreperous otherwise.

I took another lost sip of wine. I must have been quiet for a long time. "Wow, that's some tasting note," somebody said as I wrote and wrote.

I can't fathom what I'd have made of a wine like that if I drank it in my thirties. I know my affect and my language would have been even more rapturous, and that's fine; rapture is a form of gratitude. But I think the soul of that young man was by no means as lavish as his prose. It was quietly patient. At least I was responding. At least there was a spark, and nothing to block ignition. Maybe it's as simple as this: an older man drinks, and his ghost drinks with him. Then the question is, who's writing the tasting note?

During that spring there was a sequence of small damaging things. One had to do with the business and the other with my normally (or abnormally) ruddy health. I've always been the guy who doesn't get sick or who gets the weensiest version of whatever illness I do get. But during those days I got just sick enough to feel, for perhaps the first time, vulnerable. I could no longer assume that I would always prevail, at least not against the galloping crud that invaded my upper respiratory system for several unnerving weeks. When my sense of smell came back, I was transfixed by the aroma of nutmeg—I sniffed the jar of whole nutmegs to measure how much sense of smell I'd lost— as though it were a shaman of the world's ridiculous vitality. I rummaged through the kitchen like a crazy person, sniffing everything in reach—the culinary lavender, the dried rose petals, the saffron and the peppercorns and the pumpkin-seed oil— feeling almost militantly delighted. *See? I told you I'd get better.*

Being weak wasn't entirely a bad thing for me. I couldn't delay writing my annual catalogue of the Austrian wines I'd selected to offer, and I was curious to see if it would reek of a sick dude's prose. But no, it was the usual slurry. Except that in one or two places I felt the arrival of something new, something I'd never thought of or hadn't had the words to say.

It was stark. And being stark, it could seem almost brutal. I couldn't find the sugar coating. Things just insisted; experience decided not to spare my feelings. This was true although I was writing about pleasurable things. But I seemed to be receiving pleasure in a different way. Tasting the new vintage at Nigl (in Austria's Kremstal), I had every reason to feel ecstatic; Martin Nigl had the precise vintage he was *meant* to have, and the wines accumulated into a giddy parade of the microsurgical clarity his wines show at their best. In fact, I was excited; we'd waited a while for a vintage like this. But when I arrived at the sine qua non, the best Riesling, my thoughts veered away into an odd new vector. I wrote:

> Sometimes I think the portal to greatness is a kind of void. First they take away gravity, then they take your words, and when they've made you feel entirely helpless, then they let you in. Each time I drink a great wine I have the feeling "None of my tricks are any good here." All the little stuff we deploy to try and stay on top of life. In some sense we come to greatness naked, not because greatness "demands" it, but because that is its language.
>
> None of the things we agree are exalted is easy. Love will kill us. Ecstasy flattens us afterwards. Greatness strips us down before it lets us in. These things are gorgeous and fierce, and sometimes we seek comfort in that which is pretty and reassuring, and where we maintain the fantasy of control.
>
> With a great wine we begin by trying to write about it the way we do with all other wines; we show what we've seen by breaking it down. If we're delighted or amazed, we try to say why. The wine is an object we try to describe. With a great wine, our words are like tiny fists raining useless blows against a huge edifice of indifference. All we can hope to say is what it's like to *be* there. Then if you can, you say what the wine is like in some new way, and your reader is sure you're unwell.
>
> There are "easy" great wines. They overwhelm you but they're visible—incandescent, but visible. This Nigl Riesling isn't quite that kind of wine. It has the esoteric, exotic aromas I expected to encounter, but the palate is nearly incomprehensible. It alights on each living thing in a kingdom of flowers, stone fruits and herbs, releasing a massive sensual vinosity within which all the world seems to be steeping. The wine was bigger than I was. I'll have to buy half bottles!

It felt like a kind of defeat. It *was* a kind of defeat; the wine subdued the part of me who presumed it could be apprehended and then described in language akin to its particular fierce beauty. Clearly that wasn't happening. And yet I was granted access to something that felt empty, a sort of purgatory to prepare me to meet the wine in its own purity. The joke was, language wasn't needed anymore. Everything was understood, and nothing could be said. I never actually felt *more* merged with a wine, as if we'd mingled our very cells, yet I was rather brusquely stripped of all my "talent." And if I simply wrote, "This was great wine; some of you know what I mean," that's the ghost tapping out his code, wondering whether some other ghost is at the other end of the filament.

It continues. I've been finding that each new experience of a great wine seems to shove me toward a relentless severity. It isn't exactly bitter, but it knows if I tell even the tiniest lie. In *Reading Between the Wines* I wrote about Michael Moosbrugger's "Tradition" bottlings in a chapter about mysticism. Michael (at Schloss Gobelsburg, an Austrian winery I also visited) sought to enter the mentality of cellar masters 130 years ago—a kind of time travel in itself—and the resulting wines convey an aura so ethereal I wonder if the modern-wine drinker has any means of grasping them. The wines have continued to be curiously and exquisitely beautiful, but nothing prepared me for what poured from my pen tasting the most recent Grüner Veltliner: "It smells like a sorghum brine, or like a beef consommé and then a giddy popping flourish of saffron; a total *thrall* of aroma, leading to perhaps the greatest GV I've ever had."

I'd recently drunk the great 2008 and was properly silenced by it, but this singular type of wine has been growing more intricate over the years. The 2011 I tasted that mild spring day was so creamy, so musical, so grave, yet so hopeful. It wasn't sad; it was grave because life is serious. Stocks and gelées, spices and glazes, a kitchen full of stories, a home full of welcome, a respite in the unquiet life. And a funeral in the coming days, as the family gathers. That kind of serious.

I'll try to say what I mean. Not long ago my wife was ill,

and one night I was awake for a time, and I heard her lungs rattle as she breathed in her sleep. I felt first a tidal surge of love—she's sick and she's so *little*, just one little human with her rattly lungs. And then I wanted to do something, to snuggle her, but I was afraid to wake her, she needed her sleep so much, so I lay there and my love had nowhere to go. It was just my useless love in the dark. And then of course I thought of the last time I'd snapped at her and all I felt was awful; doesn't she have enough trouble without contending with bossy old me? Then I thought I'd apologize in the morning, but I knew I wouldn't. These are starry thoughts you feel while you lie there in love and ashamed and think about your ruined kindness.

This wine doesn't embody those feelings; it *addresses* them. It speaks to the you that is hidden away. What other things talk to us like that? And who, finally, is the listener?

It is your ghost self, it is the you you do not own, it is the doomed longing to unite all your clamorous factions into a single unified self, something you can describe and control, it is the rueful laughter at all the human foible, it is the grief of each thing within us that we starve and ignore. And this ghost means well by you, as long as you understand that it is honest and sightless. These days, if I encounter a great wine, the first thing I feel is *Uh-oh, here goes*, and then I don't know anymore. I used to think I knew, but beauty wants something it can ask for only in ghost language, and now we are both of us drenched in passion, my ghost and me, shining darkly and flying blind.

8
FINNEGAN'S NOTE

In the best of all worlds, when we open a bottle of wine we enjoy a delicious collision. Sometimes we meet in a place of soul, and sometimes we're just happy to have something to slop down with our pizza, but no matter whether exalted or mundane, we drink the wine and the wine drinks us. I have always been curious to explore who is who and what is what. Who is the man I've brought to this wine? What is this wine in itself, apart from my drinking it? What might we learn from traipsing around this unguarded frontier? I set about to understand, and I began with myself. As you will see, these landscapes are replete with surprises.

My day begins much like yours does, with a dream. On this day I was dreaming of a milky gray evening, in an airplane flying over Ireland ... *36,000 feet ... heading west, racing the night. The night will win, it always does ... Looking down onto the tiny places of the world, somehow even more real from this altitude .... the scene itself should convey a certain amount of loneliness, even before we see the figure on the phone in the foreground, or who enters the foreground ... I'm sorry, who is this ...?*

<Eyes open>

Ah, the room. My room. Ah, yes, I was dreaming. I suppose this is a person's first thought of each day: *That was a dream, and now this isn't a dream anymore.* Now I am awake in my bed. Next thought: *When is it?* You look at the clock. Then *What day is it?* You try to remember, and then *What have I got to do today?* and maybe it's Sunday and the Sunday papers are waiting on the porch, or maybe you're going out to dinner, meeting friends, or you're getting your flu shot. Whatever it is, it's a day.

Sitting up, scanning the floor for the slippers . . . the best days are the ones with the open evenings, at home. I seem to want to be at home more than everything else, just to make a meal and eat it at my own table. I notice that my wife has already gotten up, so I put on my slippers and grab the bathrobe and think of my dream and enjoy the by-myself-ness of even this small instant. I go to the window and draw the blinds, and the sky is large and clear. It is September, and starting to cool down. This makes me happy, because I hate summer. I have seasonal affective disorder in reverse: summer feels ominous, and it presses down on me and I get truculent and sad. Mine must be a gloaming soul. I love when the evenings come early — it is so cozy.

It is a workday, just another normal one, and my wife is already into the *Globe*. I remember that we're welcoming the cool weather with a special red wine, the kind we never drink in the summer. I stood the bottle upright yesterday.

My sweetie greets me and asks what's wrong, because I greet her absently, as though I might be mad at her, but it's only the aftertaste of that dream of loneliness, and it has me feeling pensive.

I make the tea and sit with the newspaper, and though I do this every morning without thinking or being consciously grateful, I know this is the happiest I can be. I don't need big rituals (though I like them sometimes), but I like my little ones — clearing the tea dishes, loading the dishwasher my very own way, the same way each day. It can drive a wife crazy, especially one who is by nature spontaneous, but I'll bet she approves, however ruefully. She knows I feel safe when I repeat these little gestures.

Even though I know I am no safer than any of us is, which is not very safe at all. I enact my simulacrum of safety, and chaos keeps its knowing distance.

Though the dream was hardly dramatic or passionate, something in its feeling tone stays with me. I exercise and shower and enter the world of the workday, feeling oddly tender toward my correspondents, customers, colleagues, and friends. In the middle of the day I take a break and walk in the bracing light, into the village to run some errands, and I get one or two quizzical looks, like *What's got into you?* Or, *What are you so nice about?* When I get home there's a crew down the street working on the electrical wires, and their noise is bothersome, and now the fragrance of the dream is gone and I'm feeling peevish.

Mostly I keep to myself. My wife is the sociable one. She's made friends with the neighbors. If they concern themselves with me at all, I'm sure they think of me as standoffish, or perhaps more charitably as the quiet type. I don't seem to mind being the quiet type. I've made plenty of noise in my time; I've had to. I wanted to be successful and charismatic. I wanted to be celebrated. I wanted to be noticed. I wanted to get my way. I wanted not to be forgotten. I wanted not to be abandoned. I made all the noise I had to. Now I want to be in a cloister with a bunch of birds. Sometimes I want to blast my fussy complicated prog-rock music and let somebody else make all the noise. I still have to perform sometimes, and in small doses I still enjoy it. I used to relish it. Now I manage it, and need a lot of quiet time to recover from it. I am certain I do my best work from a place of silence — even my ordinary work of selecting, marketing, and selling wine. There is a being of some kind within me whom I have barely ever known. He's been content to be an invisible power source, but he'd like to be noticed and fed now and then.

Though there were times when I was very pleased to be ignored. My paternal grandparents lived in New York City, in a place called Peter Cooper Village. This was a bunch of low-rise brick apartment buildings angled together, with mingy bits of lawn among them, all stuck between First and Second Avenues downtown. All the buildings were the same and they're all still there. My guys lived on the fifth floor in one of them, and I was taken along with my parents when they made their dutiful visits. There was a corner window in my grandparents' living room, from which one looked down a kind of tunnel between two of the apartment buildings toward the East River, and I remember very well there was a large crane at the end of it, sometimes just standing there and other times—wonderfully—in motion.

I was four or five, and like many boys I loved machines and vehicles that moved and worked: bulldozers, tractors, tow trucks, and cranes. I remember standing by that little window, listening with half an ear to the adults' conversation, entirely absorbed in the crane, and it was all the more superb because I saw it at the end of this light-filled space between the buildings. If anyone had come over to look at it with me, this would have been all right. It would have been quite understandable. *Look at that crane. Yeah, isn't it great?* Ah well, a man can dream, when you're soul-deep in the oneiric stream of memories. It's more likely that I'd have been challenged: *Why are you so interested in that crane?* And what could I have said? I'd have thought, *Am I doing something wrong?* and could only have stammered, *I dunno . . .* But what actually happened—I recall this vividly—was that one of my grandparents said, "He's sure fascinated by that crane." I may have thought, *Well, wouldn't you be?* But mostly I was glad to be left to myself as the conversation drifted along over my small shoulder.

Are we still inside a wine book? Indeed we are, because in this journey everything bears upon wine and wine bears upon everything. But if you find we've gone too far afield, I sympathize. Let's spool the thread back to wine qua wine.

I look back on this curious memory, decades later now, and I am struck by whom I now align with. It might easily have been the grownups, looking at their crazy kid lost to the world while he stares at a crane. *Huh, kids!* I could hear myself thinking. But I am no place near those thoughts; I am entirely inside that child, absorbed not only by curiosity but also by a kid's incipient grasp of beauty. To me that crane was beautiful. It is only now that I understand the gift and grace of the reverie. I am that person far more intensely than I am this person, this earnest adult attending to matters of great import and solemnity. I have never *not* been that child.

And of course this bears upon wine. Wine can open up worlds, immeasurable, inscrutable, unquiet, and sublime. You only need to be where reverie can find you.

Let me recall to you that we're looking at what happens during the day that leads to the evening that leads to the wine. I told you it is a special wine, not only a good wine in itself but also a symbol of our—okay, *my*—relief that the worst of summer is over. It would be one thing if the day sort of built a golden road to the bottle and I reached it with my anticipation intact and moist. It would be something quite different if I had a ratty day and I reached the bottle still resentful and preoccupied. We think we taste with some unmitigated objectivity, but we almost never do. To fully understand a wine we have to understand the nature of the stage that's been set for it. My little reverie about the crane will leave a residue that might make me more receptive to the wine, or to certain aspects of it. In any case, I'm a human being who is having a day, and later on a special bottle will be poured.

Oh man, I've been daydreaming. It's gotten late. I snap into gear and put in a couple hours of concentrated work, and soon I start to think of dinner.

The wine we'll drink is an old Rioja, a kind of wine I love so tenderly I almost can't stand it. We'll cook for it, something autumnal and consoling. But what is there to be consoled about? Nothing, really. I don't think anything awful or gloomy has happened to either of us today. Still, when something (or someone) offers consolation, you take it. It goes into the "general difficulty of living" box, and maybe it's there the next time you need it.

It is indeed a ceremony to greet the nascent autumn and the first cool evening with the first of the wintertime reds. But ceremonies always make me awkward and self-conscious. My wife knows we're having a *significant* red but not what it is. I'd reached into the box the day before, the one with the old Riojas, and found this bottle to stand up, not that these wines have much sediment. I stood another wine up alongside, in case this bottle was corked. A lot of Riojas of that era came from cellars with TCA-contaminated barrels, and you can never be sure. I thought about it when I brought the bottle up from the cellar. I looked at it as if to say, *So, will you do your trick like I taught you, or are you going to screw it up?* Then I felt silly and almost ashamed. So I back-spaced as if to delete the vulgar thought and started over. I looked at the bottle and took off the thin wire cage those wines have and played with the capsule. I am appallingly brusque about capsules and such; I just wrench them off the bottle. Once I got this one off, I tidied up around the rim, though in fact this bottle was almost suspiciously clean.

Yet the cork was clearly the original, and behold, the wine smelled good. I checked it above a light source to see if decanting was needed, but there was just a silky wisp of cloudiness at the bottom, and I felt happy to pour it straight from its bottle. By now this wine was the beneficiary of all my relief; it wasn't damaged, it wasn't too old, we wouldn't lose any to sediment. I started to love it before we'd even tasted it. How can you not love an old wine that's so hale and cooperative? This would be a good evening.

The wine was from Bodegas Palacio. It's called Glorioso, and though the back label says (simply) *Crianza*, not *Reserva* or *Gran Reserva*, the front label is full of flourishes such as *Cosecha Especial*. I didn't know what to think. It's a 1966, from Laguardia in the Alavesa. I bought it from a shop in Berlin that specializes in wines like this. I knew little to nothing about it. I didn't research it, because I never do. I have more fun if there's a little mystery around a wine, and I definitely don't want to read anyone's tasting note.

(In a later chapter I knock around on the topic of whether it's better to know about a wine in advance. It's a yes-and equation, because of course it's better and yet I sometimes love it when a wine is a mysterious stranger. In that case I don't want a mediator. I prefer it to be just the two of us, me and the wine, tabula rasa. This is exactly the way I like to be with people, too. One-on-one is my natural home: direct, free, electric, and even if you're just chatting or being frivolous, it never enters the nightmare of small talk. But of course an introvert like I am will have an introvert's relationship with a bottle of wine.)

I regarded it for a moment. *Who are you? How far have you traveled? Did you ever think you'd end up here? Who was there when you were born? Are you ready to interact, or are you still shaking off the dreams?* For I am very sure that wines dream, especially old ones, and they are just like us, they need a few minutes to remember where and who and what they are and to be sure they are awake and not still dreaming.

Wine is masculine in many European languages, and since I discovered this cheerful fact I have found it mingy to call a wine "it." He is a "he," and I know I've bemused countless sommeliers when I've said, "Yes, we will keep him." I tilted the bottle to pour the first glass, and he poured out rather pale but admirably healthy, not much decadence nor the tired brown of too much age. Took a sniff—*Bless him, he still has fruit!* In fact he had a lot of fruit, and not much oak—a mere *crianza* after all—but he also had an enticing panoply of suggestion, as if he'd kept a rich solitary journal over the years and was slowly parting the pages to show us. He spoke in murmurs and slowly, not because he was ill at ease but because there was nothing to shout about and no reason to hurry. He'd waited this long. Nor was I impatient; rather the opposite. I wanted to suspend this moment for as long as I could. Drinking the first few sips was like warming your hands before a fire and feeling that sweet ache as the cold starts to yield.

He was a modest wine, but that is not a euphemism for dullness. He just wasn't clamorous or assertive. He was friendly in his diffident way. If he were a person, he'd be the houseguest whom your normally shy dog loves immediately. He seemed to want us just to feel comfortable. And yet this wine began to exhale the most suggestive and enigmatic complexity, all the more poignant by being so discreet and delicate.

I could try to tell you what the wine tasted like, the usual laundry list of descriptors, or I can tell you how it was to be with it. The descriptors, I think you know, are otiose. Maybe they're irrelevant or even incorrect. ("There is no possible way a person can taste chive flowers in that goddamn wine.") But even if I nail them, then what? How much can it possibly matter to you? You weren't there. Some geezer tasted this thing and that thing in an old Rioja on an early autumn night. I don't care about that, and I'm not sure you ought to. An interesting moment that might be a story is reduced to a small, asphyxiated list of flavors, themselves zephyrs and chimeras. And all the while a larger thing transpires and is ignored.

I'm looking at the empty bottle now; it's been on my desk the past few weeks, glaring at me like something between a shaman and a pest. I know what it wants, but I'm not sure how to give it what it wants. The moment of beauty is fleeting by nature, and if you freeze it in order to depict it, then you can't also be *in* it. If you have the time, an hour and a notebook and no one to answer to, you can write along as the moments pass. But this was dinner, and my sweetheart was cooking and I wanted to keep her company. Albeit the wine was "significant."

But there was a moment when the food was reposing and we could wait a few minutes to serve up, and so we took our glasses out onto the deck, where it was cool enough to feel fresh but not cold enough to drive us too quickly inside. And we were in luck: one of the supermoons was rising—we have a few months of abnormally huge apparitions when the moon is in perigee—and we sipped the wine and looked at the numinous moon as it rose behind little midlevel stratus clouds, which it lit from behind, casting inverted white shadows like spindrift. It was a spectral vision of gray and white and cold out in the bracing September evening. Yet inside our bodies was this warm murmur of appetite and history, tactful and even affectionate, breathing a savory yet delicate umami, ham fat and cedar and all of it braising warmly, and there it was, or seemed to be, the whole arc of beauty, the chill and the awe of the moon, the haven and welcome of the wine, all arriving from very far away and all joined in this tiny tenebrous instant, the sunlight in the wine, the moonlight in our eyes.

We came inside and tucked into a homey early fall dinner, and I looked at the bottle on our table. *What were you brought here to say? How do I know I have heard you? Have I welcomed you as you welcomed me? Have we been friends for these hours?*

It is a paper-thin line between being present in the moment of beauty and writing twee little paeans concerning "the adventures of my soul among masterpieces." I don't suppose my soul's adventures matter very much. Yet I am also very sure that we must bring our lives to these moments, or the moment is wasted. And so I stand there with my life in my hands, and between us a spark occurs just like the little spark when we light the burners on the stove, and that ignition is something *we must know.* It is offered up to us, and if we're not conscious, then we can't be grateful, and if we're not grateful, then what do we have to ward off despair? Life is hard enough. And so I marshal such gifts as I have, puny though they are, and write these few thoughts about what it is to be human, and what things we can carry, as we arrive at the rim of the glass.

9

THE TASTING KNOT

In the previous chapter I tried to place the experience of drinking wine in its natural and ordinary context as the culmination of a lived day. What brought the drinker to the glass, and what did he carry with him? This seems to me like a crucial dimension of wine tasting that people—experts and novices alike—often overlook when they think about what they're drinking. It's an oversight that robs pleasure and meaning from what ought to have been—at least—a sensuous moment.

But at the same time I keep feeling that when we are *there*, about to taste, it's best if we obliterate ourselves to the fullest possible extent. I am contradicting myself, of course. Maybe it's an example of Niels Bohr's maxim that "the opposite of a fact is falsehood, but the opposite of one profound truth may very well be another profound truth." Not that I am all that profound. I am just contemplating the billions of words written about wine and trying to understand what it all amounts to and whether it is helpful or illuminating. I can't shake a dogged suspicion that it's chasing its own tail.

And what's so special about wine? We don't write tasting notes for peaches or tomatoes or cucumbers, or for corn chips or seaweed salad or Kaiser rolls. Even restaurant reviewers don't really write tasting notes when they're describing dishes. And fine, yes, I understand: every wine is different, and a peach is a peach is a peach. We want (need?) to recall what the wine tasted like. So . . . scribble scrabble scribble.

When I first heard the (apocryphal?) tale about Native Americans' reluctance to be photographed—because they feared the camera would thieve their souls—I wondered if the same might be true of wine-tasting notes. In *A Field Guide to Getting Lost,* Rebecca Solnit has a passage that reads: "No representation is complete. [Jorge Luis] Borges has . . . a story in which a poet so perfectly describes the emperor's vast and intricate palace that the emperor becomes enraged and regards him as a thief. In another version the palace disappears when the poem replaces it." As with poets and palaces, so with wine drinkers and wine. Does the tasting note describe the wine or obliterate it?

Consumers who use these notes to guide their buying choices have debated whether a single person's notes are preferable to a tasting panel's aggregate note. One publication publishes each panelist's note individually so that the reader can compare them. One wonders where the thing stops; I mean, why confine the exercise to "experts"? Why not a team with some experts and some neophytes, so that the neophyte reader (or shopper) can glean the impressions of one of his own?

One could convene a tasting panel consisting of experts in other fields: baseball umpires, auto mechanics, veterinarians, even psychotherapists. Why not psychotherapists? After all, they are trained to identify the patterns and subtexts of behavior and motivation, so why not flavor? I might rather read that conversation than the typical wine chat chasing its own tail. "I found this wine suffered from low self-esteem." "Well, what do you expect from a wine called Dismal Hollows?" The vets could be even better: "Does anyone else find this wine to be scrofulous?" Makes a nice change from the heedless proliferation of tasting notes.

I am increasingly convinced that if the tasting note is a gesture of ridiculousness, wine *criticism* is reasonable and necessary. And the critic, like the essayist, moves among her own contradictions and elisions. And so into the breach . . .

I set off intending to write about a few wines I've enjoyed recently. I wanted to get out of my own way and try to immerse in the wines as such. It isn't all that hard. I know how to turn off and become an almost pure receiver. I often do just that, as can you, as can anyone; it's a habit you establish and practice until it's second nature. The problem arises when you start to think critically about the wine, because then you can't be a pure transmitter anymore. All of you is there, and every little word choice you make is about you and not the wine. I know there's a fantasy about tasting objectively, but as soon as you start your tasting note, you can't banish yourself. Of course, if you follow this logic, a lot of wine writers and critics will be out of a job. So we try, and we agree to suspend disbelief that the thing is attainable at all.

Sometime within the past year or two I was consciously trying to obliterate myself and immerse in a wine, not to look for words but to see if they'd find me unbidden. I'd been scrolling through Leo Alzinger's 2013 Rieslings, trying to see if they're really as sublime as I thought they were when I tasted them as cask samples. I no longer feel guilty about drinking baby wines, because I finally learned how wrong it is to use terms like "infanticide" to describe drinking a wine before it's deemed to be ready. Drinking a wine isn't the same as killing it. Of course, drinking a young bottle precludes drinking that particular bottle in the future, but so what? The youngster has his virtues *because* he is so young, and we'll never again see those virtues if we wait.

This bottle was as splendid as a wine could be. I have often cited wine writer David Schildknecht's coinage describing the feeling of perfection as (paraphrasing) the momentary certainty that nothing can be better than this wine in this moment. Whether there are "perfect wines" can be conjectured — and the assigning of a "perfect score" actually clouds the issue — but there are many perfect *moments* with wines, and drinking this Alzinger was one such.

2013 Riesling, Steinertal (vineyard site) Smaragd (the top level of dry Wachau wines), his "best" vineyard, and his most celebrated wine. Among his family of Riesling siblings, of which there are four or five, the Steinertal is the least driven by fruit as such. It is rather so limey and herbal it almost feints toward Sauvignon Blanc. It is always, even in its ripest iterations, a shady wine, a thing of balsam and jade, silver rather than gold. The '13s ripened slowly and deliberately, under cool conditions, and they never attained high alcohol or peachy "sunny" flavors, yet their poise feels effortless, they are graceful as if by birthright.

Is the foregoing a tasting note? That's not what I'd call it. My wife and I enjoyed the wine together, and in the moment I wasn't writing but trying to be a pure receiver, or as close as I could come. To be open and available—or to try—allowed impressions to flow at their natural speed, unmitigated by my cogitating mind. And the moment itself unfolded with a grace that echoed the grace of the wine.

At first this wine indicated a facsimile of sweetness, not as sugar but as kindness, more a sutra than a flavor. Basically, it was delicious. Then it started a counterpoint between the energy of its herbal jive and the repose of its smiling yellow-plum midpalate, and these things kept ricocheting around like a little steel ball in a pinball machine, and just as I felt I was keeping up with the volleys I also grew aware of how beautiful this wine tasted. Just when *that* hit me I also noticed, as a heartrending coda, how tender the whole thing was. You're not amazed by brilliance from a steely, high-definition wine, but you are not only amazed, you can be melted by a wine so creamy it seems to stroke your skin and glaze your senses, yet also show an articulation of flavors so judicial and deliberate and clear that for a moment you really don't know how these things can coexist. I took the glass outside to drink in the cold fresh air and I knew there was nothing more I could ever want from a wine. No asymmetry in view, no imbalance, not even a telling flaw, just a wise magnetic friend who seemed to care for me. Later on, with a few years of bottle age, it will be less frisky, and eventually all the miracle flavors of aged Riesling will develop, yet spending an hour playing peekaboo with Baby was the best time a man could have.

We took it to the table and drank it with a seafood chowder, and it shone over and over again, as if from an inexhaustible well of benevolence and helpfulness. If it were a first date I'd have been half in love before getting up from the table. (*I don't ever want to* not be *with this person.*) Yet what seems clearest now is not how much I admired or loved the wine—though I did—but how wholeheartedly I liked it. A wine can show any number of virtues, can fascinate in myriad ways, can seduce and ravish and enthrall, but the richest feeling of all is when I wish I could hug it, because it is so wonderfully, incredibly lovable, and it makes me so happy.

We're talking about flavor, how we register and remember it. But when you're in thrall to the wine in your glass, you don't care about any of that. Some other thing is asking for some other part of you. I remember drinking the last bottle I owned of 1978 Quarts de Chaume from Domaine de Baumard. Good Chenin Blanc makes me helpless. It has many of the same parameters as Riesling—autumn fruits, smoke, minerality—and yet Chenin is almost always more implicit, allusive, and searching. I'm fairly romantic as guys go, but even I'm not sure I remain in consensual reality when I encounter a wine like this. It isn't ethereal Chenin, but it is true and in the best sense ancient and mysterious.

This '78 is a glass of evening sky. It isn't unbounded; it has borders and strictures. It isn't a father and son wondering over the great mysteries of the night sky; it is the father admonishing the son when he mistook a point of light, "Learn your stars and planets, boy!" There is a sternness here. The wine is gorgeous but absolutely unsentimental. Tough-love Chenin.

I swim in my feelings about Chenin. Even my beloved mystic Riesling is scrutable alongside these vaporous beings. As this wine sits in the glass it grows heavy-scented, deathly, like faded flowers; it is a lyric darkness like no other. It is the petals strewn over the coffin. It is the strange internal monologue of the pallbearers—*this is a grave moment, the coffin is heavier than I thought, he was my friend, I'll miss him so much, I'm sure glad it's not me in that box.* Life is awful; life is good.

What are we to make of this experience? Whom do we share it with? Is it a thing we can share at all? If I say this is a wine that simultaneously propels you to your elder-being while joining you to the virginal child you were, is this something you can expect anyone else to understand, let alone feel?

My professional palate sees that the finish is clipped and the structure is trebly, as it would be in a high-acid vintage. I can't insist it is great wine. I can only report it is a great experience with wine.

I'm glad to have visited such happiness, since I'm a reasonably sanguine fellow in general, and because lately I have been preoccupied with writing *de profundis.* We spend our lives subduing sadness, because, well, sadness is sad, and who wants to be sad? But also we seem to have learned somehow that we are obliged to one another to affect happiness, because that makes everyone feel just great, and we don't want to bring people down. Please understand, I am not talking about clinical depression but about ordinary melancholy or Weltschmerz or just appreciating the particular melodies of wistfulness. As a rule, they don't let you do that. You have to be jocund. "How's it going?" *Me? Just great!!!*

It takes a lot of energy to keep that float in the air, and these days I'm happy just to skip the parade if that's okay with you.

Even if it isn't; I've had enough of it. Time to get in touch with my scowling resting face of the soul, I think. Or at least to permit myself times of ordinary normal sadness when that's the way I happen to feel. Not grief, not bitterness, not despair, but merely a consciousness of mortality and difficulty, and the compassion that arises from letting such feelings be. Wine is no longer an entertainment for me, or not very often. It is a companion on a dusky journey, a friend with whom to be glad of the nautical twilight of things. Sometimes you just want to sigh! Sometimes you lower your shoulders and shrug away the pose. Wine is forgiving that way.

We had a 1966 Burgundy, a good bottle of Henri Boillot's Pommard Les Jarollières. It was an entirely good but by no means great Burgundy, from a great vintage, in perfect condition. A good bottle for a reverie. It was like the blood of a sad man in a kitchen where cèpes were sautéing and some Chinese five-spice was in the air. Earthy, a little feral, scents of sandalwood and soy, and immensely yet delicately sweet, as on the border of decay and not too reluctant to cross over. A little char like roasting an eggplant on a gas flame, a high note of gorse and nettle and leaf-smoke; a poignant sort of heroism, like boys playing at war. The aromas are all melting but the palate is almost gravelly, reeking of truffle and tallow, resolving into a deliberate finish of smoke and hay. Though the color is fragile, the wine is virile.

1966 . . . I took my first guitar lesson in the spring of 1966, from JoAnne Kingston. Tonight, almost fifty years later, a quarter-moon is lying on its back, innocently grinning. An old wine recites poetry from out of the glass. And where is Jo-Anne?

The wine smells like a road you want to travel down forever.

Fine old Burgundy smells, among other, more divine things, like a lover you crave so much you want to consume her. Yet you can't escape this haunting piney green, like the floor of a pine forest. Sprinkled with clove dust . . . funky and erotic and floral, like the Tasmanian peppercorns we're using to cook with. Burgundy is pagan, voluptuous and animal and mystic all at once. It needs more of you than you brought, or knew you had. It isn't coarse but it also isn't moderate. It has greedy guts. It will wrack you in its encompassing spell, its esoteric sensuality. This wine oscillates between warmth and an herbal-smoky brashness, between tomatoes engorged with sweetness and a stem of marjoram you bit into and swallowed, stalk and all.

One evening I served a wine to several guests and wished I hadn't. Not because they were unworthy of that wine—they were more worthy than I was, if it came to that—but because the wine was so noble and galvanic I wanted to be led away into its reverie. But a host has obligations, not least among them not to be vacant and preoccupied. (Sometimes I wonder if great wine is inimical to socializing, but follow that idea where it takes you and you risk sounding misanthropic.)

It was a 1959 Riesling Spätlese from Bürklin-Wolf, right in the middle of their glory days; the label claimed it was a monopole vineyard (under a single family's ownership), Deidesheimer Reiss, but these days they have no monopoles in Deidesheim, so this must have been a cadaster name obliterated by the misbegotten German wine law of 1971.* This bottle was, in every conceivable way, a great Riesling from a great vintage and a producer on top of its game. The color was no darker than pale amber, in part because there was no botrytis. But there was a vibrating panoply of fragrances—malt, leather, chest-

---

* Every bit of land in Europe north of the Alps (and elsewhere for all I know) is named. It's not Block 23, it's Daisy Dell or Owl Voice. These are the so-called cadaster names— you sometimes see "cataster" in English; "cadaster" is the original German—and I like this because naming confers a kind of respect.

nut, all in a ludicrously nuanced complexity that quickened the pulse when one considered how firm and dignified this wine was. Straw and hay came along, and the wine grew even firmer and more urgent with air. The finish was like the smoke of a smoldering hay fire, salty and estery; the whole thing was almost brusquely vital and bewitching. There was nothing that wasn't superb. Like a great Amontillado with sparks of Manzanilla salinity; it was an apotheosis of malt, not only the passage into paradise but a subsuming of the entire notion of "paradise" into some buzzing quivering sensuality, with dried apricot and milk-chocolate notes completing the seduction. It was unfathomably alive and throbbing with complexity.

That passage is fleshed out from such scribble as I could manage on the night. It was a wine that blew one's mind, that knocked one out, a killer wine, some would say—although I am struck by the violence of the language. Is there another way to apprehend such a proud and mighty wine? Can we merely observe and applaud? In all this talk of blown minds and knockouts (and homicidal beauty, I guess), I find myself picking through the words, looking for the place where joy might be. Is it there at all? Are these feelings and sensations actually joyful? Or do they perhaps address a feeling other than joy, maybe deeper than joy? Do they ask us to consider the idea of happiness in another light?

I've always felt that a great wine, as I perceive it, embodies a certain elegy, a certain sad melting, a certain force of beautiful breakdown, and that the proper response—or my proper response, anyway—is to join in its sadness. I didn't form this idea and then wrest my wines to fit it; I observed that great wines seemed always to leave me sad. I learned I was not alone in feeling this way; there's the Wallace Stevens line, "Death is the mother of beauty," but for a young person that thought is either a conceit or a luxury. It is a stern theory, and it speaks to an instinct that many people possess, but it starts to cut into one's skin when one reaches a "certain age."

It has never felt pessimistic to me; rather the opposite. I have no patience for twee lyrics to *brief vales of tears* or suchlike. I have long presumed a purpose in life and a purpose for beauty, and I view my sadness response as a call to action. That is, to consider and explore why this should be, and why it leaves me with an odd intuition, that sadness is truer and deeper and more beautiful than happiness. Or that happiness is too often and too obtusely conflated with cheerfulness—with *mere* cheerfulness, I might add. The longer I live, the less sure I am that I understand happiness in the slightest. I think I understand bliss; I know I understand delight; I'm fairly sure I comprehend states of deep affirmation in the many ways we receive it. But "happiness" eludes me, unless its definition is sufficiently fluid and capacious to include reverie, melancholy, Weltschmerz, and a tendency to dream and brood.

I admired that Bürklin Riesling with everything in me, but I didn't love it. I have loved many wines that weren't as great as that '59, and so there must be a crevasse in my emotional landscape, on one side of which wines are admired or even worshipped and on the other side of which they are simply loved. It is fairly easy to describe what makes a wine worth drinking, as we've considered, but what makes a wine worth loving?

I have an answer to that question. But with two caveats: one, that my answer is obviously not everyone's answer, and two, that my answer is provisional and subject to continual revision. That said, what makes a wine worth loving, for me, are qualities of tenderness and of a certain frailty. When I drink a proud, noble, strong wine it makes me want to play the drums. Just let me bash at something! When I drink a tender, frail wine it makes me want to read a poem or look at the moon. And it always makes me sad.

Tenderness conveys a force, and it isn't entirely sweet. It is a way we express love with our hands, our voices, our gestures, our limbs; it is a way we console, a way we appreciate, even a way we worship the beauty of another body. Yet I think the feeling is deeper and stronger than anything we can do to express it. It is never enough, whatever we do, and we always reach a point where we can't draw closer and can't express this impossible melting love by means of gestures, or voices, or even tears. And so we stare across an ephemeral chasm at our beloved on the far side, remote and shimmering. Tenderness brings us to the place we cannot join to the Other, at exactly the moment we most yearn to; it brings us to the inexorable separation of people, as though this were something love needed us to learn. And there is a perplexing sort of beauty in all this, because it is the same way for all of us, pushing up against the fractions of air that separate us and leave us alone, all of us alone, and all of us urging and pushing toward one another. And there we go on, loving.

I can't say why or how a certain wine will summon this feeling, but some of them do. They aren't the proud wines; they are the shy and kindly wines, inexhaustibly dissolving, seeming to actually love us, sweet-natured and composed. Even when they are intense and complex, they still issue this strange force of sympathy. I know I could be fiercely analytical about them, make a list of growers whose wines are consistently tender, and see what they have in common in terms of cellar work or even grape growing. I could. But I'd rather not. I don't need it explained; I just need to infer that an explanation is possible and then choose not to know it.

I imagine I'm odd that way. My checker at the grocery store has the same name as my first-ever girlfriend back in the seventh grade, Iris. Driving home today, I wondered what ever became of Iris. After a few moments of mulling and daydreaming, I realized I was happy. Happy to wonder about a girl I knew many decades ago, and happy not to know what happened to her. I've had my share of reunions with people from my past, either actual or virtual, and for each time it is wonderful there are five times when the memory is stained by the prosaic reality of knowing. Who needs to know these things? For an ordinary set of (mere) facts, you're willing to give away the mystery?

Frail wines are those whose energy is beginning to flag and who've reached this most poignant understanding: give each thing away, but hold on to kindness till the very end. Such wines are infinitely delicate but never faltering. They're unfathomably gentle but not weak. They've made their peace and are quietly showing us the peace they made. There is an echo of the old vigor. There is a whole lifetime of each lovely thing they knew, all there for us to taste and to sense. The first dog you loved as a child. Your secret hiding place. The winning run you drove in. The stories your dad read to you at bedtime. The joke you told that made your mother laugh. The first music that made you cry. The weird miracle that another person loved you back. The landscape you knew was your soul's very home. The time you looked at your beloved's sleeping face and knew you would die for her. Holding your slippery pink newborn. All of it, the sum of life with all the worry and grind removed, there in a fragile glass of wine. As the light grows pale, the divine emerges. Power emerges as strength slips away, the way stars appear from the gathering dusk.

I hope to drink more good, strong, proud wines, and of course I will, since there are plenty of them. But each time one of the other kind, a frail, tender wine, comes along and finds me, I feel it as a reminder—*listen*. These voices are heard through a cloth of years, and if I pause to listen, then they won't be lonely. And if they come to me from time to time, neither will I.

10
GLIMMERS FROM THE YEAR IN WINE

Whatever the exaltations of wine may be and whatever ruminations it may inspire, these have always been grounded in a basic professional reality. The wine has to pass muster. I need to believe, categorically, that it will delight the eventual drinker. This is so basic that I don't think about it consciously. When I am on my tasting trips, I am doing much more than simply tasting wine. I am, if I may say so, an entire person in an entire environment, consisting of landscapes and skies and villages and towns. I am looking for any possible breaks in the schedule to try to get some walks or hikes. I am driving and dealing with finding my way around—I do not use GPS. I am absorbing the many and varied atmospheres wherever I go. And to reduce this many-faceted and wonderful bustle into a sterile sequence of tasting notes seems to suck all the blood from it. I feel strongly that if I say how it *all* was, I paint a fuller picture of how the wines were.

Readers and wine lovers outside the wine industry have often asked, "What exactly goes on during these glamorous trips to European wine country?" When I was (much) younger, I'd hit the ground running, start tasting an hour after I left the airport and before I'd unpacked my suitcase, and often keep at it until the wee hours. Weeks later I'd board my homeward-bound flight, look out the window, and think, *It looks like a nice country out there. Too bad I didn't get to see any of it.* Those days are, mercifully, gone, and now I trudge along like the pensive geezer I am.

The essential point is for me to arrive at a sustainable output of energy, so that I can pay careful and respectful attention to my growers and the wines they show me. If I show up tired and grumpy, what then? They work a whole year, they line up the harvest of that year—*Here is what we did*—and they deserve a taster who is rested and ready to engage. For me, that means I don't neglect the larger environment in which their work takes place.

I don't think my customers want to buy wine from a tasting bot, so I'm going to show the larger view, the life between the tasting rooms, the whole happy schmear. Follow along, gentle reader. There will be plenty of wine along the way.

One year I was on a high floor in my hotel in Rust, in Austria, and was eye level with a couple storks' nests. This was fun. I got to see the heads of the baby storks, which you can't see from the ground. (If storks bring babies, who brings baby storks? My jet-lagged insomniac self *had* to know.) One morning I stood blearily by my window, shaking the drowsies away, and a stork was scratching its head, standing in its nest on the roof of the next house over. Rust is full of storks. They arrive in the spring and gorge themselves from the smorgasbord along the reedy shores of shallow Lake Neusiedl. Small wonder people are fond of these beautiful, magical birds, with their dreamy kitelike flight and their clackety mating calls and their silly yet beatific faces. But I'd never seen one scratch its head before; he looked like he was stumped over a crossword-puzzle clue. For a second I thought I was still dreaming. Thus began the day, a sleepy me standing alone at my window, looking at a large, lyrical bird. I felt a long way from home, and liked how it felt.

It was a short stroll across the village to meet with Heidi Schröck and taste her new vintage. Heidi makes Furmint, among other things. In fact she owns 10 percent of all the Furmint planted in Austria, and Furmint is a wine I happen to love

helplessly. It's a complicated being, late to ripen, needs to be babied, and when it succeeds it offers much to please the Riesling
or Chenin lovers. It is maybe the most purely beautiful of all
the wines I know that aren't truly great. My professional palate (such as it is) would not insist that the wines are magnificent, but my little me-soul is very sure it shouldn't have to live
without this exquisite being, even if it is ancillary. The new vintage Heidi showed me that day was subtle and entirely haunting: quince and osmanthus and bread dough, satiny and allusive
and intuitive and meditative, at least to the dream-self I brought
to the rim of the glass. It was indirectly salty with a hint of talc,
seeming to offer a sense of something you know and yet have
missed, as if you'd been at sea and returned at the very end of
spring as the blossoms were falling from the bushes and trees.
It's the wine of *saudade,* of everything known and lost, the rar-
est sweetness, and yet it lingers as if to console you. Being with a
wine like this is a lesson in how to live and what to care about. I
happen to buy it and sell it, but most important is simply to be
there, so it can find you.

Very often a few weeks or months later I see the Furmint
again, lined up with a zillion other bottles at a wine-trade tasting, reduced to a specimen for buyers to evaluate. It stands on a
table in a clamorously noisy venue, and it needs to put on some
sort of act, whatever performance it can muster under such circumstances. I don't decry this, because it's a necessary evil; how
else am I to expose my customers to these wines? I can't fly everyone to Rust. Yet when I look at that wistful bottle of Furmint, I can recall my storky start to the day when I tasted it
with the woman who made it, in her village, which I walked
across on a sunny morning under the dozens of stork nests, past
the churches and taverns and past the ATM and the newsstand
where the guy sells a day-old *International New York Times.*

Does a context like this make the wine taste better? It does
not—nor is that the right question. It allows the wine the va-
lidity of its entire environment, without which it becomes an

ever-shrinking object, denuded of its moist living pulse. To "taste" wine only takes training and attention. To *know* wine you need to know its places.

Most places become less vivid as we grow more familiar with them, but Rust is one that actually grows more curious and strange, at least to me. The Nahe region of Germany is similar. When I was there in June 2012 with the film crew of a documentary about the German Riesling culture that I directed, which came out in 2013, the Nahe felt like a soft green world one didn't so much find as accidentally slip into. Even the flowers and birds felt esoteric. The wines, which one struggles to describe, give a sense of forming a hologram of flavor on the palate, which shifts and alters with each instant of thought and gaze. You feel like you're eating food cooked by someone who has every spice in the world in the kitchen and knows exactly how to use them.

For me the place is entirely mystical. It's like the Galápagos Islands of wine, someplace where strange birds and turtles roost and peer out from heavy-lidded eyes. If you stayed there long enough, it wouldn't surprise you that your hair began changing color. The wines can have an odd shamanic force. I start to wonder, am I just slipping off the rails in my old age, or have things been pared away enough to allow me to hear what I couldn't hear before?

The eager young man who started in the wine business in the early '80s was buying from and selling to people either his age or older, but this has changed completely, and now most of my suppliers and customers are younger than I. They are very fine people, and I respect them for the aplomb with which they navigate the screwy world we've passed along. But I don't seek to emulate them. I'd prefer to find whatever odd human being lies below all the affect and dross I'm starting to shed. I learned I was introverted from a little questionnaire in a book about the power of quiet, and among introverts I seem to be off the charts. But having learned this, or even just letting the theory exist, I find myself responding more clearly to the world, and my introverted self likes introverted places. The calm, dreamy Nahe is one such.

I noticed it again one year in Germany on the Saar. Close as it is to the city of Trier, the little Saar seems entirely removed. Unlike the dramatic fjord of the Mittelmosel, the Saar runs through more open country, and vineyards mix with forests and pastures. It is deliciously relaxing. I'm remembering Hugh Johnson's famous admonition that great wine demands to be talked about. I used to agree, but now I'm not so sure. Maybe memories of the Saar have me feeling pensive, because I know that the miracle of great wine is amplified in the echo chamber of conversation among people who share this love and are fond of one another. Yet I begin to wonder about drinking wine by oneself, alone and calm, answering to no one, no need to produce affect or to contribute to a conversation. This I think is valid, too. Not always, and maybe not even very often, but just as a way to sound the inner voice from time to time. I also think there are gregarious wines and also introspective wines, and I love those autonomous little beings who don't look up when you enter the room. I have an amazingly clear rapport with wines like that.

I'm also more honest when I taste alone. Sometimes other people can spur you on, but sometimes you can't help competing, especially if you're an adolescent, which is to say a man. My notes are longer when no one else is there, and they tend to escape from me. I try to be careful and specific and concrete, but it becomes a fight against my nature. I sometimes feel as if a wine is grabbing my hand to lead me somewhere it knows I ought to go. If at that enticing point I'm furiously trying to figure out which color of iris it smells like, the wine walks away dismayed and I'll never know where we might have gone. I was too busy trying to defeat the poor wine by nailing its every conceivable nuance. I wonder who among the superbly competent young people—colleagues, producers, customers—I'm interacting with now would find these thoughts interesting, or whether they're too annoyingly vague. I only know that in wine, the true prize is not to master but to learn how to surrender. You can taste a Saar wine and write your daisy chain of descriptors —verbena-wintergreen-chartreuse-tarragon-lime-etc.—or you can say it is a walk through the deep woods with a monk who shows you what plants you can eat. Then each step is a blessing. It's like taking a fistful of edible leaves and squeezing the juice from them. The bracing spiciness is leavened by an almost creamy tenderness. I don't know how to account for such a thing. I taste it, and walk among wonders.

People my age often suppose life was better when we were young—not just our own lives but life in general. I do not thus suppose. But this much I think can be said: in the fine-wine world, today's young drinkers have even less access to the great benchmark wines than I did thirty-five years ago. Who can afford such wines now, even without student loans to pay off? I'm not sure these people even know what they're missing, because they have far *more* access to a vast world of fascinating, distinctive wines that were obscure to me then, or may not even have existed. But I feel a nagging concern that all this lavish noise doesn't permit a signal to emerge. It's just a wonderful entertainment, flattened along a horizontal plane. The great classics of wine need to exist as a foundation upon which the rest of wine stands, without which the whole edifice teeters and flutters in every little breeze. If this deepest piece is missing, then all the other pieces that balance on it are unstable and wobbly. Wine becomes just another ephemeral and incoherent thing.

I know it can seem like all these lofty classics from Bordeaux or Burgundy or even the New World "collectibles" are strictly the purview of Swiss bankers or Hong Kong plutonium magnates. How can it possibly bear on your life? It can't, yet it has to.

We need a way below the surface. When we don't have one, we start forgetting there's anything down there. We build a stunning edifice of superficial complicatedness, and when I write "stunning," it is not sarcastic. The young wine people I encounter know vastly more than I did at that age, but even then I may have known better about principles of organizations and values. Otherwise this-plus-that-plus-this equals nothing more than this-plus-that-plus-this. How do we learn orders of salience? How do we glean which things are trivial, which are worthy, which are important, and which are crucial? How do we recognize greatness when it arrives? And how do we account for how it makes us feel?

We have at least to assume there is such a thing as profound experience. It may seem inaccessible, remote, or nebulous, but someday it will find us. Some bottle will open the trapdoor and lead us down.

We are not all equally sensitive to the profound. It's facile to blame the byte culture for inhibiting this ability, but in fact I doubt it's an ability at all; it's simply an aspect of temperament. Some people possess it, and yet I have to wonder whether there's something in the syntax of modern life that obscures our view of it.

I do know that profundity takes time, a willingness to give time, an ability to slow time down, and some sense of the way time passes at different speeds. We're terribly busy compressing time into little capsules of reality; we swallow them one after another. We expel them one after another.

When we are visited by profundity, we seem to watch the propulsion of time dissolve. But if you're polishing your 'tude, you won't notice it. And a life without the potential for profundity is a diminished life.

When I began with wine, there was a lot of literature describing raptures with profound wines. I saw it as permission to feel. Quite a relief for a guy like me. Today as I scan around the wine lit I don't see very much writing about the larger values. I see people trying to be the first to break the news about some Viognier from Tobago, I see people asserting their points of view about the issues of the day, I see plenty of consumerist rankings of wines, but I see very little revelation, or even just passion. Thus I suspect others aren't seeing it either, and that may be a reason they don't associate wine with the potential for transcendence.

Obviously not all wines are profound, but just as obviously a few of them are, and when we know these wines exist, they give form and layers to our entire wine experience. Please remember, though, that profundity is the opposite of cerebral, the opposite of exciting, the opposite of entertaining by dint of its novelty or intensity. It is instead a calm cloister where our souls can live.

It can't happen if I'm hurtling around hither and yon (and speeding on the Autobahn), trying to cram in four visits on a day better suited for three, hurriedly writing tasting notes, no time to think, no time to exhale. My true life of wine is what happens in the beats between the events, when it can be absorbed and processed. Yes, of course these are tasting trips with a mercantile purpose, but they are also visits to the wellspring.

Profound experience doesn't (and shouldn't) happen often. Even if you're one of those collector guys with a cellar full of masterpieces, if you drink them too often you can get jaded.

I'll share a note I wrote a few months ago, about a wine I knew would be good, maybe even great, but did not know would be profound. It was a classic Riesling from the Rheingau, from an estate that was stellar when it made this wine.

First, it was a good bottle. The cork came out in pieces but came out, and the wine was entirely clean. We drank it at home one evening, just my wife and I, at cellar temp, about 54 degrees.

The first glass was a solid heady amber, and a little cloudy. That was fine. With wines of this age, you know they freshen in the glass, and the first impression is just the outermost layer of skin.

Bricky, spicy aromas breathed into low notes of leaf smoke, sweet paprika, and malt. The palate was (still, after quite some time in the bottle) rich and sweet, but then it became overwhelmingly estery, with Palo Cortado orange peel and nuttiness. The wine was berserk with intricacy and beaming with confidence —it wasn't broody or meditative. Then came a milk-chocolate note like the ones old Champagnes are wont to show. This wine was solid and stentorian, yet part of it was melting, or seemed to want to.

But that's okay; I'd melt for us both. I took the glass outside into the February cold, under a cloud-riven moon, and there came a celestial fragrance of lime parfait, a new green note, and the green swooned into the orange swooning into the paprika and rust, as if I were observing an old poet working on something difficult. The force of expression felt crucial, like the things one says with the final breaths and the grieving loved ones at the bedside. But the wine itself didn't feel tragic or sepulchral; it was flourishing and robust.

The second glass was colder—I'd wanted to lower the temp a bit—and was even more estery and malty and felt less sweet. It was truly great wine, an aching dark zenith of loveliness, malt sprinkled over tenderness sprinkled over death.

And yet! It was still itself, or rather, *he* was still *himself,* a riverfront Rheingau Riesling with the classic dried apricot of Hattenheim. The "old" wine thing shimmered at the edges like the overtones of pealing bells.

It was a full-grown adult. It could easily go another fifteen or twenty years. It was a Spätlese from a great vintage that would peak around age seventy. *Seventy!*

A 1959 Hattenheimer Stabel Spätlese. Estate-bottled Schloss Reinhartshausen. I was in Miss Nordeen's kindergarten class when those grapes were picked.

These days we'd be microanalyzing the acids and extracts and looking for reasons on paper why a wine or a vintage might be considered excellent or great. We'd busily explain it. In those days, people just knew. It was clear in the vineyards; a grower once told me, "You know when a vintage is great when the whole floor seems to rise, when you don't have to 'select' to get great wine, but when the whole thing's on fire." The 1959 was such a vintage, yet if it came along today, we'd fuss that it doesn't have enough acidity. Maybe the young wines seemed sweet and flabby; I don't know, I wasn't there. But I did see the laughable way many of us in the trade misjudged the great vintage 2003—not all the wines, certainly, but that small segment of profound ones. And I think part of the reason we failed to suss out '03 is that we weren't taught how to read and recognize profundity.

Of course this is all well and good, but how do you know? How *do* you recognize the profound, or distinguish it from the merely remarkable, amazing, or stellar?

First, the wine pushes you away from itself. Right away you find you're not thinking about the "item" in your glass. You're thinking about your life. Sometimes you're just thinking about *life.*

Then you find it hard to break down the flavors, not because it's actually difficult but because it seems irrelevant. You're too busy looking for someone to hug. You want to hear music, or read poems, or just look out at the moon. You don't want to fart around with descriptors.

I've already referred to the curious sadness that seems to walk along with profundity. In part it is the residue of another unsettling feeling, that now, this minute, you are in the country of reality, that what you thought was your life is only so much flotsam.

Another gift of profound wines is to seize your imagination and hurl it a thousand feet into the air. There are views you haven't seen before. If you have to write, write *those* things down. Then peer back at the innocent bottle and nod a small thanks for appearing and showing the way to the sky.

I wonder sometimes at this "spiritual" quirk of mine. Having been adopted as an infant, I delved through the literature of that situation as a middle-aged man and learned that the abstractions surrounding adoption are conducive to an ethereal sensibility. Put another way, the unreal is something of a home for us. Another thing I discovered was that adoptees tend to romanticize connections, especially those of blood. Both things are true for me; I am quick to respond to the mystical, and I am stirred by connection, yet none of this is reducible to my particular circumstances. That is, I do not make these things true but instead am marked by a gravitational pull toward them.

Connectedness became a trajectory into the potential for profundity for me, and it's a little glib to say it became my basic soul-business. What actually happened was that the whole thing kept kicking my ass until I had to respond just to make the pain go away. Fundamentally, disconnected wines simply weren't valid, and the facsimile of "significance" they affected was irritating. It damaged and disoriented our capacity to discern, because two things looked real but only one of them was. And so my little adopted heart insisted on authenticity and sought to show how it might be recognized.

This business, if you will, is ever more urgent, yet I am finding it sweeter to urge it quietly. It lives its truest life in quiet places, as I do. And one such place is Uerzig, on the Brunnenstrasse, where Rolf and Alfred Merkelbach are living out their lives making Mosel Rieslings as they have always been made.

Earlier I saw their tale—the bachelor brothers working their tiny domain—as something colorful and cute. The two of them are adorable. But eventually, slowly, over the years I visited them, I'd find myself weeping (quietly!). Something very beautiful was being enacted here, and I needed to listen and see what it was. When we filmed there for my 2013 documentary, I learned that the 1,100-liter casks in which the wines are made and aged, and whose numbers often appear on the labels, are often specific to individual parcels, so that cask #12 always houses the same parcel's wine. *A connection.* The camera guys weren't sure why I found this news so delightful, so I tried to explain; each vineyard has its own barrel. Okay, there's a thread between *this* parcel of vines and *that* cask. Yup, got it. It's almost like the cask is *seasoned* with that small vineyard's wine. Yes, we understand what you're saying. Look, it's as though the cask *remembers* the wine.

As if such a thing could ever be! But why not? Stranger things happen, such as two brothers around eighty years old not only continuing to work a steep-slope estate but actually *buying* vineyards when something irresistible comes along.

One year my visit to Rolf and Alfred was my second appointment of the day. My *commissionaire* Johannes Selbach's wife, Barbara, was there, along with their son, Sebastian, who joined several of my visits in order both to taste and to observe us tasting. He was at the stage of wanting to taste everything, a stage I know well; patterns seek to form, and he wanted enough perspective to discern them. In these instances, the less I say, the better, because it's preferable for him to have all the white space he needs to make it be his, not a simulacrum of mine or anyone else's. So I merely asked if he'd ever tasted Merkelbach, and he said he hadn't.

Both Rolf and Alfred were ailing. Some shitty virus was going around Germany, and everyone was hacking and light-headed. As we sat at the tasting table, poor Rolf's lungs were so wheezy it sounded like a cat was meowing to be let into the room. So the brothers were subdued, and looked their age.

Originally, decades in the past, they worked a barely two-hectare estate all on steep slopes, divided into about thirty-five different parcels. In the interim, finally subdued by time itself, they've reduced the size of the domain by about half. They've also become known, thanks in part to my earlier book's German translation. The secret is out—at least the superficial secret. They still do it all themselves, with part-time help for harvest and for exceptionally busy times in the vineyard cycle. They don't cut grape bunches away during the growing season, a yield-reducing practice known as green harvesting—believing it's a sin against providence—and they don't pick selectively in multiple trips through the vineyard to pluck the chocolate chips from the cookie. If you know the en-bloc series of wines at Selbach-Oster, in which three parcels are left to the last possible moment and then picked in their entirety, you'll be interested to hear that all of Merkelbach's vineyards are picked that way. Just like always.

In 1978, when I first visited these Mosel villages, they were full of tiny estates like this one, every little street festooned with signs to taste and buy direct from the grower. Today there are fewer growers, and they've gotten bigger as vineyards have come onto the market from luckless neighbors who were closing their doors. Merkelbach was typical of the artisan production structure of an earlier time, and they haven't changed. But the times have.

Now these bigger estates have to compete for a slice of a smaller pie, as wine is no longer a routine everyday beverage but instead a drink for specialists and aficionados. An active press has arisen to lead such drinkers to the best stuff. As soon as you establish rankings and hierarchies, you induce growers to examine your criteria and adapt their wines to them. It's human; it can hardly be helped. So everyone's wines are pimped up to get the scores they need and to land on top-ten lists. Everything's richer, more concentrated, sweeter (if sweet at all) and more alcoholic and imposing (if dry), and so the entire grammar of wine has changed entirely—except for a small few holdouts like Merkelbach, who aren't even aware they *are* holding out, or what they're holding out against. They're just making the wines they've always made, honest, true, fresh, and light-bodied Mosel wines.

After the first wine was tasted—a Kinheimer Rosenberg, as always—I told Sebastian Selbach these were ur-Mosels, something essential and close to the wellspring of this thing's identity. It sounds ridiculous to say they make me feel young again, but they have a way of collapsing time, so that the first whiff of the first glass takes me back immediately to my formative, virginal experience of these wines back in the late '70s. That smell is why I loved them. That smell is like no other smell. The purity and modesty of that smell and those flavors are a return to an Eden of bliss. As modest as the wines may seem, they possess something that makes them impervious to corruption, whether from the enticements of ego or from the temptations of falsity. I raise the glass and the decades dissolve like the foam on a glass of Champagne. There it is again; there it always is. The fragrance isn't huge, but it contains the sum of love and gratefulness for a lifetime in wine—theirs mostly, and in a small way mine, too.

Of course this is important in the downslope of my life. One is paring down. The fundamental things apply—but where does one find them, and what do they apply to? I'd argue that these things are even more important to young wine drinkers, for whom authentic experiences are all too uncommon and obscure. And when they are found, one senses the enactment of a pastiche of authenticity. Even when the wines are truly authentic, when are they ever as beautiful as these modest little Rieslings from Merkelbach?

And when are they ever this accessible? Rolf and Alfred have barely raised prices in twenty-five years, for *truly* small-batch, handcrafted wines done on such steep land that no machines can be used. Did you know that nearly all their vineyards are ancient ungrafted plants, some between eighty and a hundred years old? Can't you imagine that if such wines came from some more fashionable place, they'd cost exponentially more?

I hope I am wrong, but I suspect that for many new young wine lovers there are so few authentic things left in the world that they hardly learned how such things might be recognized. Anyone could lead them to some young hottie making sexy-pants wines and being active on Twitter, or to some crusty old coot in an austere and forsaken corner of Spain or Italy who's making wines whose obscurity is, let's say, understandable. (We get seduced by the story, but the wines are iffy. Come on, admit it.) So if anyone thinks I'm just flying my silverback flag by dedicating a life's work to two white-haired guys whose wines haven't changed a lot in thirty years, I think there may be aspects of the world you don't yet understand.

As we sat there tasting each new vintage, I felt again how unadorned these wines are. They are faces that need no makeup. They're articulate but never chattery. They are completely beguiling but never seductive. They are full of substance and yet weightless. They taste eternal and yet also eternally fresh, as though the gravitas of slate were dancing with a gurgling, cooing innocence. Even other wines I *like* have more affect than these do. Merkelbach's wines are pure life force, and I cast about trying to remember when I'd ever tasted anything like them. And then it came to me.

Sebastian Selbach had grown pensive, and I leaned over to him, saying, "You know, these are the kinds of wines Hans, your grandfather, made, and these are the kinds of wines that formed his paradigm of what Mosel wines actually are." He gave me a searching gaze that nearly undid me. Souls moved about the room.

Rolf and Alfred have also seemed to condense a million pages of Buddhist study into two divine and simple lives. They need very little and are thoroughly happy. They love their lives, and though they're starting to consider what might happen when they're no longer able to work their vineyards, each time they step near the brink they pull back—"Oh, we're not ready to give it up just yet, we'll just do it as long as we can." Think about it: Do you know anyone who is leading the exact life he was meant to lead? Someone who is unreservedly happy, whole, integrated?

I can name two people.

In contrast, something I like about working with young vintners is the multitudes of little kids in the vicinity. The year after we shot the documentary footage, as I was driving along the Mosel on the way to Graach and Willi Schaefer, I reflected back on the scenes we had in which both Willi and his now-grown son Christoph said the same thing: as children they played in the vineyards when their parents worked, and later they wanted to help with the work and were very proud to be useful, and they observed a paradigm of happiness when the work was being done, and so it was little surprise when they wanted to carry it on as adults.

After we tasted we sat down to dinner. The kids had been put to bed hopefully, but Jakob, the younger boy, wasn't sleepy, and came padding out to join us. He was full of smiles. The child smiled at everyone and everything, at his parents, his grandparents, his toys; I don't know when I've ever seen a more loving little kid. It made me wonder and it made me a tiny bit sad. It could have been that way for all of us, if we'd just been more affectionate, maybe. Maybe. Schaefers just make it look easy, to love and be happy.

Willi and I had gone down to his old bottle cellar to pick out some wines for dinner. He left me alone at one point. I thought of being there alone, with access to anything I wanted to drink from the cellar of a universally beloved vintner and an old friend. I suddenly felt very shy. I was absurdly unworthy, yet there I was, unworthy me, threading my way among the bottles.

Six weeks later I was in Austria and it was the full profusion of spring. I was alone that year. My colleagues were otherwise busy, either working or getting to know their newborns, so I went about by myself, as in the old days. The one-on-one with growers was different, and I relished it: more deliberate, quieter, less guarded. And my time in the car between appointments was mine alone, so I could think and introspect and listen to my notoriously dreadful music.

I got to Feuersbrunn an hour early for my visit to Bernhard Ott, so I seized the caprice and went for a walk. Leading toward the hills was a road lined with ornamental cherries, all in bloom, heavily scented on the mild humid day. The vineyards were full of clovers and grape hyacinths and other little bloomers whose names I didn't know. It was the lunch hour, and very quiet; when the 1 p.m. tractors started up, the noise would be jarring. But for now it was peaceful as I walked along.

I saw rabbits, deer, and pheasants in the vineyards. To a wine grower these creatures are pests they grudgingly accept; they like the animals themselves, but they bother the work and the vines. Yet it was all so free, somehow—no one there except me and the hundred flowering trees and the rapeseed fields and the grape hyacinths. The two deer were huge, as they are when they have no predators, and when they leapt away from me it was on powerful sinewy legs.

So I got to Ott happy and full of oxygen. Before we tasted, he wanted me to hear a tape of his son laughing. The boy is seven or eight, something like that, and something made him laugh and not stop, made him keep laughing so that each laugh generated another burst of laughing, and that gurgling little-kid laughter was so wrenchingly gorgeous and also strangely sad, the life force and the innocence inevitably to be lost. Ott played it again and again, and not only because it was funny.

Little Rosalie came into the room, now two and a half but still Daddy's girl, still snuggling into his shoulder and peering out every few seconds to make sure nothing crucial was happening that she might miss. After ten minutes or so she was fetched, and as she toddled away she turned and waved a jaunty goodbye—*See ya.* A Swedish woman who works at the estate, who'd been pregnant the year before, had her baby now, little Magnus, four months old, whom she carried in a snuggly on her belly: a curious child, who regarded us quite intently, as if we were creatures he would need to consider at a later time.

As we were wrapping up, a little group had gathered—some of Bernhard's helpers, though one hates to call them "helpers" because they're really just fellow workers with roles to play. Would I like to taste a few old wines? Yup! On earlier visits I'd been shown the important wines, the monuments, and Bernhard certainly didn't need to demonstrate to me that Austrian wines could age. At first he brought out very simple wines from old vintages, the kinds of wines no one really kept around because it was presumed they needed to be drunk young. This is always fascinating, and I loved the wines, but I wasn't surprised. What *did* surprise me was a succession of wines, many of them in half bottles (which usually decay a lot more quickly), consisting of grape varieties his father grew, such as Malvasia and even Müller-Thurgau—both, again, assumed to be fragile—and these wines were astounding and uncanny, not fresh exactly, but neither were they flagging or limping into oblivion. Bernhard himself was amazed, and his team didn't know what to make of this unlikely parade. I watched my host as the bottles persisted and saw a beautiful thing. Bernhard was as flummoxed as we all were at the vigor of these old wines that weren't supposed to have made it this long. But even more, he was gathering a kind and loving pride in the work his father had done. Of course these wines were heralds of another time, and of course the times had utterly changed, and yet! I watched the thoughts steal over him: *It didn't start with me; people in this house have been caring about wines since before my time . . . My dad was okay even with grapes we don't grow anymore . . .*

Do you see? The wines themselves fell into the group of Wow. Who knew? Really-cool-to-have-tasted-*those* oddball items—yet no one would have rated them highly if judged as mere wine. But they were something much larger and deeper than mere wine. They were a pure gesture of origin: vinous origin, family origin, human origin. I looked across the table at my host, laughing and talking with the team about his father's time, and I thought, *This is how a man lets himself be known.*

When our "work" was finished, we went outside for a *jause.* This is a snack of simple food one eats in the open air. It entailed raw-milk butter, delivered twice a week along with raw organic milk, cream, and yogurt. (Ott's son complained one week, when the supply had to be supplemented with organic milk from the supermarket, "Did you thin this with water or what?") There was half of a huge wheel of mountain cheese from a high-alpine maker they know personally, and two big blobs of blood sausage made by one of their workers, Patrick, and some raw ham Bernhard had carried back from the Italian Alps, and some bread baked twice a day by the woman who watches the village kids, and at one point someone observed, "You know where each bit of all of this comes from," and Bernhard said, "Yeah, I guess I do." It was him and me and his gang and eventually also the guy who manages the compost and another guy who does the grunt work in the cellar, who turned out to be the guy who also made the blood sausage. A little world.

At one point a little boy arrived on his bike—he may have been eight—looking for Ott's son, who was still at soccer practice. Bernhard said, "Marcus will be here in a few minutes. Come sit with us and have some food," and so the kid removed his helmet and took his place. They told him what all of it was —the cheese from the pal in the mountains, the ham brought back from Italy, the bread baked by Mrs. Someone, the butter from the guy who delivers the milk, the blood sausage from Patrick—and what was so stirring about it was that the boy was an entirely valid citizen, treated as an equal, spoken to like a player in the world of affairs, not like some puerile *kid* but also not precisely like an adult. I watched, amazed—how exactly do you bring this off? You do it by talking to him as a *human being* who belongs among you, even though he is young and small, and this boy spoke back from his rightful place, not as an imitation adult but as a boy with equal status. I really was gobsmacked. I mean, there we were, sitting under the sky on a spring evening, eating this lovely food, being human beings together with the blackbirds singing and the evening coming on, and the child was not even exactly invited but rather included because of course he'd be included—what else would he be? His pal was coming back in ten minutes or so; hang out with us while you wait. I thought, *This is how you raise whole human beings; just like this.*

I was a little weepy when I drove away. It seemed like I had somehow misplaced or lost my life, or had disregarded it. What I'd just seen had looked so easy. I wondered if it was as easy as Bernhard made it look. I don't know, and I wish I knew. It would help me to know. As I drove on through the darkening country, the lilacs had started to open, and in a still-sunlit field was one of the many small religious monuments dotted all over Austria, out there by the road. It was Christ on the cross, but this particular place had been allowed to grow wild, and the lilacs were up to his chest, profuse and fragrant, and I thought, *This is how this day ends,* Christ on the cross, covered in lilacs and blood.

Not many days later I sat under the champion linden tree in the courtyard at Nikolaihof in the Wachau. It is said to be the oldest known wine estate in Europe, yet there is nothing solemn about the people or the wines. The linden tree is legendary; if you've seen it, you haven't forgotten it. It's become something of an emblem itself, that fine being, yet at heart it's also a kindly giver of shade and shelter from the rain, not to mention a home to a lot of birds. One can't imagine Nikolaihof without that tree, yet one also can't quite explain why it makes such sense. It seems to coalesce a lot of love into its nexus, that huge green soul. The birds love it, the buzzing pollinators love it, any person who gets near it loves it, and I'm sure the tree loves its life and being beautiful and useful. There was a moment when proprietor Nikki Saahs's little wirehaired dachshund, charmingly known as Lumpy, was up on his tiny hind legs peering intently into the tree and barking, and Nikki explained, "Sometimes when we throw his ball to him it gets caught up in the branches and eventually falls back down, and Lumpy thinks the tree is also playing with him." Well, *that* explains everything.

11

WRITING DOWN THE BEAUNES

In March when I make my annual tasting trip to Germany, the only flight from Boston (where I live) to Frankfurt is a Lufthansa nonstop with the absolute shittiest possible schedule. It leaves at 4:15 p.m. and arrives at 5:20 a.m. the next day, just when I'm starting to feel sleepy, and now I have a whole honking day to get through. It's still dark when the wheels hit the runway. The airport is deserted, the kiosks all boarded up, only a desultory handful of bleary-eyed workers are starting to arrive to open things up. Newspapers are roped in piles outside the stands. By the time I'm through passport control and have gotten my luggage, the car rental place is still closed, and I have to stand around in the cold waiting for the early shift to show up. Eventually they do, carrying their coffees and hoping for a few minutes of peace, only to have it cruelly broken by a stumbling customer with bloodshot eyes. I'm amazed they give me a car at all, since I look like some undead and harrowed being toting a suitcase.

I climb in and try to figure out the unfamiliar vehicle—I'm sure if I press the temperature-control button the trunk will pop open or the mirrors adjust—and I look for some hyper music to keep me awake. Finally I pull out and onto the almost empty Autobahn; only the all-night trucks and a few stray commuters keep me company. I'm heading to Nierstein, where the Strubs live, which takes about twenty minutes from the airport at that hour. The dawn gathers behind me as I head west.

When I reach Nierstein it's a surmise of daybreak, the bakeries are turning their lights on, and bags of warm rolls tumble out into display baskets. A few moms are walking with their kids to school. Traffic is building, the streetlights flicker off, doors to growers' courtyards are heaving open, and only the brightest stars are still in the sky. If the winter has been mild the blackbirds are already there, and as I drive through the village toward my hotel I open the car windows to hear them—it is one of my beloved sounds, and seems to welcome me to Europe. If my room's ready I shower and walk over to the Strubs', where Margit will make me a pot of strong tea. We catch up on the news of the village as I rub my tired face. There will be no tasting this day; it wouldn't be fair to the growers, as wiped out and dehydrated as I am. I used to do it in my younger, more macho days, but one outgrows such things.

Still, it is Day 1, Nierstein is awake, and I walk back to my hotel to get into the car and drive to a nearby city to keep busy —the stimulus of a city is helpful—and eventually the day begins to wane, and I grab an early supper and hope I'll sleep through the night. Work starts the next morning. Even those growers who know they're seeing me on my first tasting day are probably rueful, if not resentful, that I'm there with half my wits, but someone has to come first, and I know my body and how to allow for its condition.

It has been three decades of early March arrivals and early morning arrivals, and some days are gray and low while others are bright and cold, and I enact my little ritual yet again as the day gathers and little Nierstein opens its eyes.

I had a lot of time to think over the course of that bleary day. I thought about why I was buying more socks when I already had too many pairs of socks—classic jet-lag thought! I found a hotel lobby I've always liked and sat with a pot of Darjeeling and the *International New York Times*. I enjoyed the yellow and purple crocuses that sprouted on the sunny lawn outside the entrance. I thought of me in my wine world again, and felt both immersed and very far away.

The teapot was empty, the paper was read, the socks rustled in their bag, and so I drove back to my hotel and turned out my lights and collapsed into sleep.

The next day, while I was tasting in Nierstein with my old friends the Strubs, an interesting thing happened. One wine was a dry Riesling called Taubennest. Taubennest is the cadaster name for the best parcel in a site called Oelberg. And this wine taught me a valuable lesson.

What follows is my tasting note, in which I do what tasters do: deconstruct and analyze the flavors of a wine, and also the progression of those flavors and the way the pieces fit and flow. In so doing I felt that the finale of this wine was a little mordant, and this disturbed me *in the context of tasting*. But the same evening we took a bottle with us to dinner, and at the table the wine was wonderful, because all it needed to show was its mass of fruit and mineral as it entered the palate. I didn't hyperfocus on the finish because I didn't *notice* the finish; I was either stuffing food in my gob or talking with my friends. So the question seems to be, which is more true, the way a wine tastes as you "taste" it or the way it drinks as you *drink* it? That wine was seriously enjoyable at the table, and my inner voice admonished me to not be such a damn pill about the finish.

I think this clash of purposes is maybe here to stay. My job as a merchant is to taste and to share the results, but we need to understand and agree that this stuff is only true in a *partial* universe, the Judgments of the Tasting Room. In the whole universe, where we simply *use* wine for any of its numerous purposes, the judgments may not pertain.

In that spirit, I suggest that this wine is very dry but that it is also the opposite of thin or meager. Its terroir aromas are massive (sandstone over slate), and it has some of the capacious earthiness of (dry!) Alsace Riesling. The palate is juicy and rich.

That's all: juicy and rich, imparted by the old vines in this parcel. *Then* it seems to slink away a little, and the last flavors are unyieldingly stern. Yet even then the tertiary finish is solid and deep. The wine is strong and significant; in the tasting room it felt a little miserly, yet at the table it felt delightful. I'll recall this wine for its fine moments and hale companionship, and the little nitpicks I discerned matter a lot less—though they do matter. A certain asperity on the finish is a frequent feature of the 2015 German Rieslings, which are otherwise quite sound. But just when you think they're being chummy they lash at you with a sardonic quip, and you think, *One doesn't entirely relax with these wines.*

I've started to be the last guy on the scene with a pronunciamento about the latest vintage. Some generalities can be made, of course, but anyone who needs to know exactly how great these wines may be in the aggregate is asking a knave's question. Most of the time you just can't know. Once in a long while, maybe every fifteen years, a crop comes along that seems to be manifestly outstanding, but when you call it "great" at that moment, you're talking about the euphoria you yourself accumulated and not so much about the wines. I have a rueful memory of a German Pinot Noir about which I was wrong not once but twice.

It was a '99 from the Pfalz estate Müller-Catoir. The cellar master, Hans-Günter Schwarz, was seriously proud of the wine. And the three encounters I had with it from cask were compelling, so much so that by the third encounter I was ready to call it the best German red I had tasted to date. I think I offered it in 2002; it may have been earlier. It seemed to herald a new realm of possibility for *German* Pinot Noir, not something imitating Burgundy but something expressing itself without reference to any benchmark.

So I praised it to the skies. And it was bottled. And after it was bottled, it didn't taste very good.

Fine, I thought; it's ordinary bottle sickness. It'll come

around. And yet it didn't, and each new time I tasted it, it still didn't. Man, I had some serious words to eat. The wine was stiff and fruitless. I spent most of my time tasting white wine; what was I doing trying to be an authority on some weird-ass German Pinot Noir?

But in the greater scheme of things, it was just one little lonesome wine. It would disappear. And even though I had some awkward conversations with customers who couldn't find the manifold virtues I'd claimed to have discerned in this beverage, I hoped my cred would survive.

I bought four bottles for my private stash. The first two weren't fun at all. I decided to keep the last two for a few more years. If the poor thing never came around, I'd marinate some stewing beef in it.

Finally one year the wine started peeking out. It was still a small version of the euphoric thing I tasted from cask, but at least it was wine again. And then, at long last, ten years after the vintage, the final bottle was opened. And then I wished I had *more*, because this wine was starting to soar. Bastard took its time! It had become a really serious Pinot Noir, with a German firmness of spine and a certain rectitude about the fruit, but with texture and vinosity and length.

Schwarz never let the wine undergo malolactic fermentation, that is, a bacteriological action occurring at or just after the end of primary fermentation wherein the wine's (harsh) malic acid is converted into (smooth) lactic acid. Remember, he didn't seek to imitate Burgundy. His only compromise was to age the wine in large neutral wood instead of the stainless steel he used for his whites. Maybe that's why the wine was so taciturn after bottling. But however one explained it, or tried to, it was cheering to finally taste the wine I'd so praised. Cheering, and unnerving.

I'm not saying this because I was relieved to be vindicated. If I affect indifference to being wrong, I have for the sake of simple decency to be equally indifferent to having been right after all. No, what I'm really after is to demand the right to clamor.

Not exactly to clamor for answers but instead to clamor for the *questions to be heard.* I know that wine is always better from cask; I allowed for that. *Why* did this wine vanish after bottling? *Where* did it go? Is there a way to have picked the lock to unearth its flavor? *What* might it have been? Should I have been less impatient? And finally, how much do people actually understand what a guessing game this all is? To be sure, the longer you taste and the more experience you accumulate, the more educated your guesses are. But will readers (or buyers) meet you there? Or must you feign omniscience in order to be credible at all?

I had Schwarz's cell phone number, and if it weren't the middle of the night in Germany I'd have called him and kvetched like hell. "You might have warned me your '99 Pinot would disappear into a shell."

"Well, kid, I might just have done that," he'd probably have replied, "if I myself had known. So instead let me welcome you again into the worrisome uncertain world. It's awkward as hell, but you tend to meet very honest people here."

I visited one of my Champagne producers, Jean-Baptiste Geoffroy (of René Geoffroy in Aÿ), and again it happened, a fine old wine that connected to the deeper threads of living. We often conclude our work by tasting an old wine or two, and we knew the first bottle was an old (then called) Cuvée Selectionnée, a mostly Pinot Noir *cuvée* now known as Empreinte. The bottle had come from the cellar of a M. Pierrot, who was "like an uncle" to Jean-Baptiste and who had this wine in his cellar when even the Geoffroys themselves didn't have it. "We opened one of the bottles several months ago," said JB, "and it was the best bottle of our wine I've ever had."

Well, then.

The color was a noble pale gold, and the aroma was heart-stopping, sweet and fine and pure. I have detailed elsewhere the panoply of achingly beautiful aromas of old Champagne, so I won't repeat them here. I also *can't* repeat them, because just at this moment we learned that M. Pierrot had died the previous summer, eighty-one years old, and now my pen was stilled.

When I could write again, I wrote, "Forests in heaven ought to smell like this, some aggregate total of leaves and peace and happiness." The wine grew spicy and powerful, even incisive, and all of us guessed, correctly, that it was a 1976, that power-house vintage, still stern and growling.

Another wine arrived, and we already knew it was an '82 Cuvée Prestige (today's Volupté), and it smelled divine, limpid and as sweet as a just-caught trout. The palate was orgastic. Salty, sapid, verdantly ripe, endlessly savory, oyster shells and even still a spine of freshness, a wine in the utter prime of its life and entirely great. The previous (and only) time I'd tasted that wine was the evening of the day I first met JB and his wife, Karin, back in 1996 or so, when we joined them for dinner. I guessed its vintage then and JB thought I was a savant, but vintage aromas in Champagne are uncannily like vintage aromas in German Riesling, and I know those in my bones. So, nineteen years apart, two encounters with a rare and haunting beauty.

Word's gotten out that we like old Champagne. "We" in this case consists of me and whichever motley scrum of sybarites comprise my entourage, though that word is heinously unfair to several of them, whose knowledge of Champagne is greater than my own.

There aren't so many of us. The glories of mature Champagnes are the wine world's best-kept secret. You almost never see them on wine lists or at auction. I'd like to think there are thousands of bottles slumbering peacefully in cellars in Britain, but I wonder if that is true anymore. The big houses in Champagne do keep archives of great old vintages, but I'm just a lowly country wine merchant and am not vouchsafed those opportunities. So the chance to taste old Champagne is something I seize upon, and when I talk about it everyone assumes it's just weird old me bloviating about some other bit of wine esoterica.

Among wines that age, there are two possibilities. One is actually fairly routine; the wine preserves itself very nicely and changes a little but not a lot. (Most ordinary commercial wines should have a best-if-drunk-by date on the label somewhere.) Among these wines are favorites of mine such as dry Muscat and Scheurebe, the best examples of which will keep quite well for up to fifteen years, albeit they barely taste different at fifteen than they did in their early youth. The second possibility in wine's developmental capacity is far more interesting; there are wines that seem to undergo an entire metamorphosis, changing over decades into mysterious beauties one had no reason to surmise. To cite a blatant example, my main-squeeze Riesling has mature flavors that cannot be inferred from how it tastes when young. It is almost unique in this way.

If you put two glasses of Champagne in front of even a decently experienced wine nerd, and one was old and the other was the wine you could buy today, and you said, "True or false: these are the same type of wine," most would answer false. Because there is no intuitive or sensually logical chain whereby this turns into that. You need to have tasted old Champagne. And you need to have learned that these northern wines possess a curious gift of apotheosis.

But the next wine was entirely interior and mystical. It was a vintage wine from 1961, herbal and nutty but without the compound-butter flavor some old Blanc de Blancs can show. I started writing descriptors (scallion, arugula) and then got mad at myself. I mean, who cares? So I let the ambient chatter dissolve into a pleasant kind of noise and just walked through rain-drippy woods until I saw a trapdoor, and this led into a cool green ether where all the souls were floating and gazing, and I looked into my own soul and it was empty. The moment seemed designed for a big full soul-belly, but for that moment, and for whatever eccentric reason, I was only looking on.

It bothers me that you can have these experiences only vicariously, and I'd understand if you felt that they didn't pertain to your life. Isn't it vastly more important for a wine to taste good when most of us will actually drink it? Of course it's important. But it is actually more important for certain wines to show us the reason for their journeys, what lies at the end and what's along the way. It is the pinnacle of what wine can offer, and if it doesn't exist (or if it isn't cherished), then wine loses its North Star, its guide beacon, and caring deeply about impoverished wine seems a little fatuous. If wine cannot inspire, it draws closer to all the other consumer commodities in the world, and if there's anything more inspiring than these resplendent old wines, someone please say what it is.

When you're lucky enough to drink wines like these now and again, you can forget, while the trance washes over you, the risks and efforts entailed in making wine. A couple months later I was in Austria to taste and make selections, and the first day was behind me, and I took to my bed. In the middle of the night I was woken up by lightning. It had been a clammy day and hadn't cooled off much, but I've known hotter twilights, and no storms had been forecast. But it was quite the light show, flashing almost without pause for several minutes. Since I was now wide awake, I broke the rules and went to the window to watch the storm. The gust front blew in—I heard it whoosh through the trees, stop when it passed over the Danube, and start again in Mautern, where my hotel was around the corner from Nikolaihof. The rain started sheeting down, a few small clatters of little hailstones, and then in five minutes it stopped. So I went back to bed and listened to the consoling sound of retreating thunder, and enjoyed the petrichor smell and the cool new breeze.

The next morning at breakfast, there was news. The storm had only clipped Mautern, but at its boiling core it cast a five-kilometer swath of golf ball–sized hail, and over three thousand square kilometers had been affected. Worst hit were the Kremstal along the river, and then up into the Wagram, and in these places not a vine had been spared; it was a wipeout, 100 percent damage. This would affect Berger and Ott, whom I'd see the next day, and also Ecker, whom I'd already seen.

No one could remember a 2 a.m. hailstorm, let alone such destructive magnitude from a storm that came out of nowhere. A grower, a farmer, anyone who depends on the caprices of nature for a livelihood, learns to be stoic. But what I saw on the faces of my guys was numbness for their own losses and sympathy for the poor battered vines and their defenseless green shoots.

I asked a couple growers if their insurance would cover the losses, and most of them said yes, to some degree. But they would rather have had the wine. They would make do financially, but they live to make wine, and what would they do with the looming year stretching emptily in front of them?

You do what you can. The life of a small family vintner may be beautiful, but it isn't always pretty. The late Joe Dressner once told me he felt I was guilty of romanticizing the family wine estate. He felt that way because plenty of family wine estates are environmentally careless, and others make ordinary wine. Joe may have thought that my extolling the virtues of artisan wine was just a form of marketing, but for me it isn't, and never can be. Instead it's a first principle, a touchstone value that needs to be in place before the other values can be considered. And I do think—I will always think—that small-scale family viticulture is a beautiful way for humans to organize their lives. The results may not always be meaningful, but very few meaningful results are achieved in any other way.

But enough about that. I wish for a world where we could presume such things, and so I have selected a segment of enterprise where such things can be presumed and then forgotten. But in order to forget, we must once have observed, and so I draw attention, and then I back away.

I think the tastings of that year reached a pinnacle one morning in Champagne, when Didier Gimonnet did something he's rarely done and opened a duo of mature wines for my col-

leagues and me. I was surprised, flushed with joy, and quite unprepared. Because these just come at you. It's not like you've
made plans to open a couple really special wines some evening,
and you look forward to it all day, and the moment comes and
you're expectant and keyed up and you're already happy. This
was the middle of a normal working day. We had appointments
ahead of us. I didn't expect this to happen, so I was entirely un-
done. I was in full working mode, walking my wine-pro persona
and mindful of the time. Would we like to taste a couple old
wines? Really? Yes, of course; that would be nice.

We didn't taste them blind for the purpose of guessing; we
did what I do with guests at home, tasted the first sip or two just
to focus on the signal and then learned what the wine was. The
first bottle in the middle of this sunny spring day was *stagger-
ing,* and even without my being keyed up with anticipation, the
wine enveloped and consumed me. It was Gimonnet's *millesime
cuvée* Fleuron from 1979, among my most beloved Champagne
vintages, and it was incredibly sweet and melting and gorgeous.
Thirty years on the cork, and probably bottled with nine grams
per liter of residual sugar—can we *please* stop being such damn
puritans about residual sugar?—it is an entirely divine thing to
drink.* Didier said, "We drank this for my wedding in 1990."
Now it has classic old Chardonnay flavors, powerful and tender, all "yellow" as '79 is, but this one's rather grandiose and
mezzo forte; an endless finish of lemon rind and Comice pear,
smoke and espresso. A wine that limned the tiny line between

---

* Someone once said that if a person knows absolutely nothing about wine, he knows
one thing—that dry is better. He may not know what "dry" means, or might like a wine
he thinks is dry but actually isn't. The endless debates and discussions and jihads around
sweetness in wine are entirely useless wastes of time. Sweetness is sometimes called for,
and when it is, the rule should be as little as possible, as much as necessary. Imagine if
there was some sort of jeremiad against salt in food (not for its health ramifications, but
because it had been seized upon for the sake of making value judgments). Salt in food is
like sugar in (some) wines. It is a flavor enhancer. We don't salt a dish so that it will taste
salty, we do it to awaken all the other flavors. Sugar in wine is similar; it can (and should)
be a crucial element in harmony and complexity.

mystical and sentimental—and I don't mean sappy or mawk-ish, just the things pertaining to affection and joy.

There was another bottle, and I think Didier must have known somehow what my most cherished vintages are—or they were his, too. For this was a 1966 Fleuron, and this wine dissolved all the walls and left you crumbled and disassembled. Smoky and smelling of wet forests and history and desire and sadness; have I ever had anything more beautiful? *Is* there any-thing more beautiful? Ah, it's the birth year of Didier's wife. Lucky woman.

A thing like this delivers your whole life to you in a fleeting vision of divinity. And then it goes deeper and reveals the eager, hopeful, sad, and grateful arc of all our lives, the delights, the longings, the fears, and the loves, the moments of eerie meaning, the reveries and absorptions and empathies, and the gratitude, for the darkness that gathers and this sweet, sweet earth. The soul is a riddle and each of us is a fathomless question, espe-cially those closest to us, whom we assume we know. But what do we know?

That '79 that's still on the table, that is knowable; it's love and beauty and love *of* beauty. "This is what I love about her." These are ways she makes me happy.

It's different with the '66. That wine is a slow-growing beam, yet fragile and flickering, trying to light the unknowable. And the light makes it visible but no less unknowable, even as it snakes through your senses and perfumes your interior, but when it arrives and shuts the door, it has come to live with the self you do not know, the you you don't possess. It's the wine of rifts and absences, of numinous emptiness; it is the wine of one lonely bird browsing through your grass, of looking out the window and an hour goes by. With the '79 the self dilates and exults; with the '66 the self dissolves. One wine makes you want to stand up and testify to everything you love. The other guides you very far away from words and shows you some of the many things that can be known but not described.

Yet even as I felt saturated with a sense of belonging, an insistent voice compelled me to challenge myself: Am I being sentimental? Am I too prone to being led by my sense of the mystic? These are nice things, of course, and I've expended many thousands of words insisting they are valid and real. But one's own truisms may be the hardest to see, and these days I seem to have obtained some avatar of sorts who wants to challenge everything I've been saying. Does this really bear upon wine at all?

I ask myself, what if we could remove every aspect of wine? What would we be left with? By "aspect," I mean all the facets and elements of wine's existence. The silly ones and the bogus ones to start. We could begin with things like "points" and "lifestyle accoutrements" and strange gross body-builder wines. What would wine be, stripped of all these things?

But we can't stop there. We also have to be willing to strip away even the good aspects, the ones we argue are what make wine meaningful, all the things I love to fuss over, connections to soil, family, culture.

We're not discarding these things because we no longer believe in them; we're doing it to try to see what wine is when everything about it has been stripped away except for its flavor. If I want to spend tens of thousands of words describing all the "larger" virtues wine pulls along with it, I ought at least to be willing to consider how wine would look without them. What happens then, when wine is denuded of all context and all larger values?

Let's hoist a glass of wine either not knowing or not caring that it's a herald of a culture, a liquid emblem of a family's fulfillment, the "blood of civilization" or some such thing, a marker for Home — basically all the stuff I've been fussing about for nearly forty years.

I take those things as givens when I drink wine, or so I might insist, and I'm not consciously thinking of them in the least. You could say they are not discretely present. Does this matter? In fact I think not, because that's a luxury I think I have earned and which has risked becoming a conceit. I'm not rejecting these values; I'm asking what, if anything, lies below them when we have shoved them to the side. It's *das Ding an sich*. Empty my mind and consider wine as such, per se, and tabula rasa.

Close off my heart, send my soul out to buy toilet paper, and consider what happens then, when you drink the mere, isolated wine.

Hmmm . . . well . . . first it has a flavor. It delivers a sensory, sensuous experience. Flavor. The flavor reminds me of other flavors, sometimes of different fruits or herbs . . . basically, food. That in turn makes me think of eating, appetite, pleasure taken in the slaking of hunger, and the taste of appealing foods. Of appealing in general, being drawn toward a pleasure source. Finally of seduction. I mean, this is all free-associated, not logical. It starts with flavor; it's an aesthetic moment. It is the pleasure taken in an appealing flavor. It doesn't relate to thirst, and it isn't sad or happy. It has structure and it shows an organization of its components, but it doesn't have rhetoric, it doesn't create an argument or make a case, and while the flavors have a beginning, a middle, and an end, they do not *persuade* unless I've approached the wine skeptically and then it turns out to be pleasurable.

It's just flavor. But it wakes me up. That can't be helped. Unless I deliberately ignore it, as soon as the flavor enters my mouth it also enters my mind and my imagination. It creates a kind of electricity. If it's a simple flavor, then I respond simply. It's nice: move on. If it's a lovely or charming flavor, then I can't help but pause, because in that instant I want to steep myself in delight. I luxuriate in it. And of course the mind wants to have its say, which is the pivot point of this little game. Try as I might to banish "mind" from this activity, my thinking faculty will try to determine what the wine is, where it comes from, how it compares to other wines, how much I enjoy it. Can I confine my mind to just observing, without trying to understand everything? Is this useful, illuminating, *possible?*

In general, the fastest way for my higher analytical functions to be banished is when a flavor is so beautiful I am overcome. Then the close-by world really does seem to dissolve, and a vastly larger world enters. Space and time collapse, noises are quickly silenced, and even subjectivity seems to know it's not wanted. A flavor of great beauty is a *moment* of great beauty, and these moments seem to contain everything, every place and every moment, simultaneously; something vast enters me until even the being I think of as "I" is nowhere—the self has left the building. And as the beauty pours in, I see that you can't strip these things from wine, because they are, if not inevitable, then inherent, even ineluctable. I feared I was risking pretentiousness, yet now I'm struck by how durable these ideas seem to be. I have sought to strip them away, afraid I was presumptuous, and yet they crowd back in.

A simple wine is a nice little tap on the shoulder, a better wine is a warm bath of satisfaction, a very fine wine is a means to be grateful that all of us were built for this experience, and a great wine is an unfathomable and sad and ecstatic illumination.

And so we come full circle: it's that final thing, the *tristesse* and regret, that seems to intensify with age. If I had such experiences in my thirties—*if*—then it was a lyrical moment and I tried to spin melodies and harmonies around it. Then you get older, you start to learn the price of tenderness, you start to understand that grief has a key to your door and you have taken life for granted. Now when I have a great wine it has *already* swept past all my external values, even those I defend and go on defending. It's like the flying dreams I had as a child. It is the one true life, the magic life, seeming to have chosen me alone, until the sun comes through the window and I open my eyes. What a ride that was! Who cares if it wasn't "real"? It may as well have been. Can flavor return your dreams to you?

The moment of beauty also has a way of suspending time, which is something that gets more important as one leaves one's youth. When I was younger, I might have passed a person—in my vision it is a man—sitting on a park bench, doing nothing. And I would likely have felt, *What a drab and wretched life.* It wouldn't have occurred to me that he might be waiting for a friend to join him. It would certainly not have occurred to me that he was happy just sitting there. We reach a point at which it is crucial to slow it all down, as we're viscerally aware of what life is hurtling toward. We grow sensate to elegy and requiem. It is also crucial to slow oneself down, and an afternoon passed in idle peace, observing the vague and urging world, is a vision of paradise. A beautiful mouthful of wine is a message from the soul: Slow down enough to take things in. Life is quite absorbing if you're not zipping through it.

I love to hike in the mountains, so much that it's hard to get me to slow down. I'm so happy and it's so fantastic that my body wants to move, to exult; if I knew how to dance, I surely would. My wife is wiser than I and appreciates the value of pausing. And of course we pause to eat our lunch.

One day we hiked above Zermatt, on one of the eastern flanks of mountain close to the Monte Rosa massif. It was a grand walk—all of them are in that blessed neighborhood—and finally we reached a stunning viewpoint with an entire icy mass across from us: Monte Rosa itself, all its fellow peaks and the icefalls that tumble down from them into the enormous valley glacier. We'd walked a way down the path toward the Monte Rosa hut, mostly to get away from the gawkers who'd ridden up on the Gornergrat train, and soon we found the quiet we'd been seeking, so we scrambled up onto a grassy hillock twenty meters above the silent trail to spread out our glacier picnic.

There is a moment when one bites into a spurtingly sweet peach while looking square onto a scene of ice and snow, when two ends of the world strain to unite, one of them warm and sweet and the other remote and lifeless, and if you've ever supposed you were "good with words," try describing this, writer stud. I was mulling over how indeed that could ever be done when a lone hiker made his way up the path from somewhere behind us. He wore a bright yellow coat and had his pack slung almost raffishly over one shoulder. He may have been hiking to the Monte Rosa hut, one of the most remote in all the Alps, involving a glacier crossing and a lot more technical skill (not to mention intrepidness) than we possessed. If he saw us on our hill above the path, he didn't let on. He did, though, pause at a point down the trail to just look out at the mountains.

I found myself riveted. Was he alone because his companion wasn't in the mood to hike that day but he wanted to take advantage of the final day of good weather? No, that wasn't it. He seemed to be carrying a certain loss with him, and the absence of that person also rode on his shoulder. They had always planned to take this hike, and now she was gone and he took it for both of them. Or they had taken it together and now he had come back alone, to reassure her—it was all still here. I was absolutely sure, as I watched him gaze over the distance, that he was talking to somebody, and listening to somebody, a woman he loved who would never come here anymore. Or a father who had told him, "My only regret is I never walked that trail to the Monte Rosa hut."

The man in the yellow coat was finishing something. But it could never be completed, this thing. It isn't in the nature of love and loss to seal off the wound and keep walking. All you can do is to walk with your ghosts and let them watch you fail, and hope they love you for it.

Presently he started to hike again, down the long trail above the glacier, and by now we were both watching him, my wife and I, and we watched him for a long time until the trail rounded a distant corner and he disappeared at last. It was heartrending to watch him in his jaunty yellow coat, hiking off into the frozen spaces, getting smaller and smaller until the brooding distance swallowed him, a small soul in the huge world.

They are beautiful and frightening, these things that tear us open. It is hard to withstand them. It doesn't feel safe. They leave us altered, a little uneasy. Sometimes we wish we didn't need them.

Splendor without loneliness is merely scenery. The deepest beauty doesn't make you joyful. The deepest human need is not to be happy but to be purposive. Beauty is a gift that comes with a summons. Find out what your ghosts want of you. If they want you to sit on a park bench and observe the theater of the world, then do that. If they want you to strap on the pack and shrug into the yellow coat and take them for the loneliest walk imaginable, then do that. If they want you to cry when you drink a searchingly beautiful wine, then it's best you obey. You cry for the beauty and for the life you're wasting—the life we all are wasting, running after joy, always running, as if joy will rescue us from the menace we seek to outrun. It will not, nor will anything else, but what helps is to stop, eat the peach, and look at the white summits, gaze out over the glacier and talk to your absent loved ones, or sit on the bench and let the ordinary world in, and bring your dancing, grieving soul to beauty when it finds you and asks.

For a book as acquainted with ghosts as this one, I dedicate the work to two of them, both beloved and always near.

To the memory of Felishia Foster

And to the memory of Jerome Joseph Theise

A NOTE ON SOURCES

The epigraph quote appears in Rebecca Solnit's *The Faraway Nearby* (New York: Viking, 2013). The Tom Spanbauer quote in the introduction appears in "Dangerous Writing," *Poets & Writers,* January/February 2016. The Pam Houston quote in the introduction is drawn from an interview with Jodi Scheer Hernandez in *The Haberdasher,* April 9, 2015. The Richard Lischer quote in chapter 7 appears in *Stations of the Heart: Parting with a Son* (New York: Knopf, 2013). The Rebecca Solnit quote in chapter 9 appears in *A Field Guide to Getting Lost* (New York: Viking, 2005).

ACKNOWLEDGMENTS

I don't see myself as a professional author but rather as a wine merchant who likes to write and enjoys the good fortune to have published a couple books. Thus I always feel a certain disbelief that anyone concerns him/herself with my writing, and does so with care, warmth, and skill. All this for little me?

It starts with my agent, Betsy Amster, whose counsel has always been wise and who is so warm and funny.

I have been blessed with a truly extraordinary editor, Alex Littlefield, who has pored over this manuscript as if with tweezers and a scalpel and made it into a far better book. His detailed concern has touched me greatly.

Ivy Givens gave us a pair of wise eyes at the perfect moment, when I was too immersed in the trees to be able to see the forest anymore.

Liz Duvall is a writer's dream of a copyeditor, especially a roughneck writer such as I. Any remaining infelicities in the book are probably just me being stubborn.

The team at HMH is outstanding, and I am grateful to Breanne Sommer, Jessica Gilo, Allison Chi, Lisa Glover, and especially to Deb Brody for believing in this book.

I owe an immense debt of gratitude to my colleagues at Skurnik Wines & Spirits, who ably kept the boat afloat when my writing spilled over from nights and weekends and into the workday. Two people stand out: Valerie Masten-Bonné and Gabe Clary.

Karen Odessa Piper is my biggest darling, and Max Theise is a way better son than anyone else has, so there.